T0128113

PORTRAIT OF A
WORSHIPER

Text Book Series

PORTRAIT OF A
WORSHIPER

HOW GOD CREATED AND DESIGNED US TO FULFILL OUR PURPOSE

SHAMBLIN STONE

WESTBOW
PRESS®
A DIVISION OF THOMAS NELSON
& ZONDERVAN

Copyright © 2018 Shamblin Stone.

All rights reserved. No part of this book may be used or reproduced by any means, graphic, electronic, or mechanical, including photocopying, recording, taping or by any information storage retrieval system without the written permission of the author except in the case of brief quotations embodied in critical articles and reviews.

Scripture taken from the King James Version of the Bible

Scripture taken from the New King James Version®. Copyright © 1982 by Thomas Nelson. Used by permission. All rights reserved.

Scripture quotations marked (NIV) are taken from the Holy Bible, New International Version®, NIV®. Copyright © 1973, 1978, 1984, 2011 by Biblica, Inc.™ Used by permission of Zondervan. All rights reserved worldwide. www.zondervan.com The "NIV" and "New International Version" are trademarks registered in the United States Patent and Trademark Office by Biblica, Inc.™

Scripture quotations marked (TLB) are taken from The Living Bible copyright © 1971. Used by permission of Tyndale House Publishers, Inc., Carol Stream, Illinois 60188. All rights reserved.

Scripture taken from The Expanded Bible. Copyright ©2011 by Thomas Nelson. Used by permission. All rights reserved.

WestBow Press books may be ordered through booksellers or by contacting:

WestBow Press
A Division of Thomas Nelson & Zondervan
1663 Liberty Drive
Bloomington, IN 47403
www.westbowpress.com
1 (866) 928-1240

Because of the dynamic nature of the Internet, any web addresses or links contained in this book may have changed since publication and may no longer be valid. The views expressed in this work are solely those of the author and do not necessarily reflect the views of the publisher, and the publisher hereby disclaims any responsibility for them.

Cover artwork by Larry DeTienne © 2017 Shamblin Stone. All rights reserved. This book was professionally edited by Joy Metcalf. All photos, tables, charts, and graphics contained in this book are © 2017 by Shamblin Stone. All rights reserved.

ISBN: 978-1-9736-1303-9 (sc)
ISBN: 978-1-9736-1304-6 (hc)
ISBN: 978-1-9736-1302-2 (e)

Library of Congress Control Number: 2018900231

Print information available on the last page.

WestBow Press rev. date: 07/25/2018

Chris Stone

Dedicated to
my wife Chris,
whom I married
May 10, 1973,
in Wichita, Kansas

Dedicated to

Table of Contents

Pictures and Graphics

List of Tables

Preface

How I Committed Suicide
by Shamblin Stone

The Origin of the Name "Shamblin"

"Shamblin" is my middle name. I have the same full name as my father, but my mother refused to let him call me "junior." Therefore, I am Ralph Shamblin Stone II. My wife, Chris, and I named all of our four children Biblical names. Our children from oldest to youngest (pictured right to left on the following page) are Jeremiah David, Hannah Joy, Micah Matthew, and Sarah Hope.

My dad received Shamblin as a middle name to honor the beloved family doctor who delivered him. Shamblin was the doctor's last name.

Rev. Ralph Shamblin Stone I 1927-1977

When I was fourteen years old, I informed my mother that I did not want to be known as "Ralphie" any longer. Although she respected my wishes, and began to call me "Ralph," my aunts and uncles didn't.

The Stone Children

"We can't call you 'Ralph'," my Aunt Lorene defended their decision. "You and your dad will never know who is being spoken to."

"That doesn't matter," I insisted.

"Well, what do you want us to call you?" my Aunt Donna asked.

"I'll go by my middle name," I announced confidently. So from that day forward I began going by Shamblin, even though Aunt Lorene still delighted in calling me Ralphie to the day she passed.

I didn't realize it at the time, but this struggle over my name was a reflection of a bigger issue in my life. I was searching for my identity. I wanted to know who I was and what my purpose in life is.

My Double Life

I grew up in an Evangelical, Christian denomination, through which my father was an ordained pastor. I was known as a "PK," which stands for "Preacher's Kid." PKs have a certain reputation for being the wildest ones in the church youth group, which I eventually lived up to.

The churches in my dad's denomination were strong believers in invitations – or altar calls, as other denominations call them – at the end of every sermon. There are three distinct components to most invitations. The first is always an appeal for people to come to the altar to receive Christ as their personal Savior. For an example of this, watch an old Billy Graham Crusade. My parents always told me Rev. Graham got his start in their denomination, before he went independent. I, however, have not been able to verify that.

The second invitational component reflects that denomination's unique doctrinal balance between the Calvinistic and Armenian positions on salvation. It was for backslidden Christians to get right with God by rededicating their lives to God. As a young teen, I did my share of "getting right with God," with tears and kneeling at the altar.

The third appeal of these invitations is usually for people to come forward and join the church.

Another distinction of my parents' denomination was a high priority on winning the lost. Because of this, the extent of their discipleship of new Christians was to equip and inspire them to win souls. Even when sin was preached against, it was done by telling us how sin would ruin our testimony.

The other pet subjects of this denomination seemed to be tithing and the pretribulation rapture of the saints. Because of all this, I concluded that true Christians witness to everybody they see about Christ, stay away from sin, gives tithes and offerings, and are watching for the second coming of Christ sometime in the next five years.

Furthermore, I understood that all of these "Christian duties" had to be accomplished by a Christian's own willpower. Therefore, I concluded that, the stronger the willpower, the stronger the Christian. After I would rededicate my life to the Lord, my willpower usually gave out in about two weeks. Then I would feel guilty that I wasn't a better Christian.

I found that living with all that guilt became impossible. I would then give up trying to be a Christian for a while and give myself to all types of secret sins. I did this to try to numb the guilty feeling I had. The only problem was that these secret sins only made the guilt worse.

I didn't know it at the time, but this continual guilt I felt actually invited demonic confusion into my life. Because of that confusion, I began to doubt that God even exists. To hide what was going on inside me and to please my parents, I acted at church the way I thought a Christian acts. However, when I was at school or with non-Christian friends, I tried to act like them, to investigate their lifestyles.

I justified my dual life when I observed the lives of the people in my dad's church. During testimony time in a church service, these people would stand up and say things like, "I thank God I have peace in my life!" None of them appeared to have peace in their lives. It seemed to me that they couldn't be a Christian any better than I could. To me, they were just acting the part of a Christian at church and living like the rest of the world during the week. As an arrogant teenager, I observed this when I was in their homes, hanging out with their teenage kids.

When I saw this apparent masquerade these adults were putting on, I said to myself, "I'm a better actor than any of them, so that means I can be a better Christian than them." At church I acted as though I had the strongest willpower of all so as to appear to be a good Christian; but inside, I longed to know what truth is and who I really was. In public, I played the parts I was expected to play. But alone, I questioned God's existence and the purpose for my life.

Joining the Air Force

I was also facing another dilemma as I reached my late teens. The Vietnam War was in full swing when I graduated from high school in 1966, and the military draft was making sure every young man above age 18 was inducted into the army to serve in that war. I successfully avoided the draft for a couple of years after high school by attending college in Springfield, Missouri. I only attended one year, but it took the draft board another year to discover I was no longer in college.

Any military veteran from the World Wars through Vietnam knows what a "greetings" letter is. It is a letter from the draft board ordering you to report for a physical exam on a particular date. Of course, if you pass the physical exam, you receive a second greetings letter with a date to report for active duty.

For me, the inevitable finally happened, and I received my first letter from Uncle Sam. That night I was totally depressed, so I decided to hang out at a party I had heard about and get drunk.

"What's wrong with you?" one of the hippies at the party demanded.

"I got my draft notice today," I whined.

"Bummer!" he responded. After a short sympathetic pause, he spoke again. "Hey, man, do you know what you should do about that?"

"No. What?" I responded without enthusiasm.

"You can really 'stick it' to those guys if you join up before they can draft ya!" he said proudly.

"What good will that do?" I looked at him dumbfounded.

"Well," he explained slowly, "that will allow you to choose the branch of service you go into, instead of being stuck in the army as a grunt in Vietnam."

In my altered state of mind, that actually made sense to me. The next morning, I went right down to the air force recruiter and joined up. After I signed the papers, I found out that if I had let them draft me, I would have only spent two years in active duty in the army. But since I signed up, I was required to spend four years in active duty. I'm still looking for that guy who told me to enlist!

Actually, I really didn't want to be in the army and carry a gun. I hated guns! The only gun I ever owned was a BB gun. One day, when I was a teenager, I was shooting that gun and hit a bird in a tree, killing it. I never touched that gun again, hating the thought that I had killed with it. Because of that experience, I was willing to pay the price of two extra years in the military in exchange for not having to carry a gun.

After basic training, however, I received orders to be an air force security policeman, guarding North American Aerospace Defense headquarters in the mountains near Colorado Springs, Colorado. When I got there, I was issued a gun to carry.

Borderline Atheist

Once I was in the air force, I was away from my parents, so I made the decision to no longer live a double lifestyle. Whatever I did from then on, I determined, I would do it with everything I had.

Since I had already tried the religious lifestyle, I dove headlong into everything the world had to offer. My cigarette habit went from a half pack per week to a pack and a half each day. I drank beer and wine every night until I passed out, and on the weekends, I did every street drug I could get my hands on. I was still looking for my identity in all of these things, hoping I could find myself by doing them.

After about eight months at Colorado Springs, I finally told my sergeant how much I hated guns. He sent me to a psychiatrist at the Air Force Academy, who told me I wasn't crazy like my sergeant had thought. The doctor told me, "You're just as sane as your sergeant."

I knew I was in trouble then.

The psychoanalysis led me to be cross-trained in a different career field. The air force made me an administrative specialist, which was essentially a clerk or typist. So whenever wide-eyed youngsters ask me what I flew in the air force, I tell them I flew a typewriter.

Then I add, "I was a desk jockey!"

By the time I changed career fields, I was a full-blown atheist. However, just because we don't believe something, does not mean it isn't true. I didn't know it, but God was pursuing me, because of my mother's prayers.

God Proved His Existence to Me

One night after drinking quite a bit of alcohol, I was laying on my bunk in my barrack's room, having one last cigarette before I went to sleep. For some reason, I started staring very closely at the burning end of my cigarette.

"Why am I smoking?" I asked myself. I never wanted to smoke—I only started because I wanted my friends to accept me.

At that moment, I remembered a time as a young kid riding in the car while my mother told her friend a story. Until that moment, I had never thought about this event since it happened.

My mother and her friend were discussing someone who was addicted to cigarettes and his struggle to quit. She then told about someone else who was also addicted to cigarettes and tried to quit several times without success. In desperation, he finally prayed and asked God to help him quit. According to my mom, he never had a cigarette after that prayer.

I put out my cigarette, turned the light off, and lay in the dark for a while thinking. Then I threw caution to the wind.

"God," I said under my breath, "if there really is a God, make me so I don't want to smoke."

I went to sleep without setting my alarm, so when I woke up the next morning, I realized I only had five minutes to get to the office. I never ate breakfast in those days, but one thing I never missed was my first morning cigarette. However, that morning I had been rushing so much that I didn't get one.

As I was working on the morning reports, I remembered I hadn't had a cigarette yet. So, I shook out one from my pack and lit it up. When I took a long, first drag on the cigarette, I became immediately nauseous, and it was all I could do to keep from throwing up.

"What is wrong with this cigarette?" I thought, as I held it at arm's length. I tried it again, and I barely kept the contents of my empty stomach down. I had to work, so I let the cigarette burn in the ashtray till it was almost gone. Before I put it out, I tried it one last time. With that puff, the nausea increased worse than before and took longer to settle. Bewildered, I snuffed out the cigarette and continued to work.

Twenty minutes later, I shook out another cigarette, not remembering the prior nausea, and lit up. This time I immediately reached for my round metal trash can and dry heaved.

"What is going on?" I yelled in my mind. "Every time I take a puff of smoke, I want to throw up!"

Then I remembered my prayer from the night before. "Could it be God is real and He answered my prayer?" I wondered.

I really craved cigarettes for the next several months, but every time I thought about lighting up, I remembered throwing up. Besides, even the smell of someone's cigarette would make me have to leave the room where they were smoking or else I would throw up. I have never smoked another cigarette since that day.

I learned two things through that experience: First, God is real, and, second, God always answers prayers specifically. What I wanted was for God to take the desire to smoke away from me, but what I asked for was to be made to not want to smoke. He didn't take the desire away; He only made me not want to smoke by making me feel nauseous every time I smelled cigarette smoke. Who says God doesn't have a sense of humor?

A Confirmation that God Exists

I found myself facing a three-hour test to finalize my change from a security policeman to an admin specialist. The air force gave me a two-inch-thick training manual to study on my own time and a test date three months away. I was warned that if I didn't pass the test, I would be back in the ranks of the security police that same night. I needed to pass that test, because I would be getting orders for Vietnam soon and I could not bear the thought of carrying a gun in a war zone.

Every night I had good intentions of studying the manual, but things always came up. For instance, friends would come get me to go drinking, and by the time we got back, it was too late to study. Night after night and weekend after weekend went by full of good intentions of studying the manual, but I never cracked it open once.

The night before the test was no exception to my irresponsibility. Friends had stayed in my room till 12:45 a.m. I was drunk and tired, so as soon as they left, I turned out the light and went to bed. I was almost asleep when I remembered the test at 0800 in the morning. Panic gripped me! I couldn't study that night—I wouldn't be able to stay awake. "What am I going to do?" I worried.

Then I remembered the miracle God did with my smoking habit. Desperate, I decided to put God to the test once again. "God, if there really is a God, please help me pass this test tomorrow." With that I drifted off to sleep.

When I arrived at the test site in the morning, I learned there were three girls and another guy taking the test with me. While waiting for the test to be handed out, one of the girls began to brag that she was sure she was going to ace the test, because she had spent every free moment for the past two months studying the manual.

She asked us, "How much have you studied for the test?"

The others reported having sacrificed their time as well to study the manual.

"I've even given up my Friday nights to study," she continued to boast. "I've read the book three times cover to cover!" She paused as if to expect me to boast and try to outdo her.

At that moment, the sergeant entered the room with our tests. "You will all get three hours to complete the test," he began in a monotone. "If you don't know an answer, skip it, and come back to it later. If you still don't know it, then take your best guess. The air force only requires that you score a 30 percent to pass. When you are finished, bring the test up to me, and I will score it for you."

Those three hours were an eternity for me. I hardly knew anything on that test. I guessed at almost every answer, if I even understood the question. Some I didn't have a clue what they were talking about, so I just randomly marked any answer for those.

I got through the test in about two and a half hours but just sat and waited. I did not want to be the first one to have my test scored.

The girl who had bragged before the exam was the first one to take her test to be scored. The sergeant silently went through the process of marking and calculating her score, then looked up at her and said, "I'm sorry miss, but you only got a 25 percent." Her jaw dropped, and she sheepishly went back to her seat, as I slid down in mine.

"I can't believe it!" she kept saying to herself.

Next, the two other girls went up at the same time and handed their tests in together. The sergeant marked one test, then the other. Then he reported that they both got 15 percent. He also made a point of stating that he found it suspicious that they both missed the exact same questions and that they had sat next to each other during the test. However, since they had failed, he would not pursue an investigation into their possible cheating.

Then the other guy took his test up to be scored. After a long silence, the sergeant looked at him and said, "I'm sorry, but you only got 5 percent correct." When I heard that, I slid down even further in my seat.

The sergeant looked at me and said, "Are you done?"

"Finished," I responded, meaning I was on my way back to being a security policeman.

"Well, bring me your test," the sergeant ordered.

My knees were visibly shaking as I walked to the front of that classroom and handed him my test. I stood as the others did and watched in ominous silence as he went through every page of the test. He then counted, and did some calculations. Without saying a word, he wrote an 85 percent at the top of my paper.

I was stunned! God had proven Himself to me again in a way that there could be no question that it was God who did it. He had bailed me out of a jam, even though I did not deserve it, just because I had asked Him. I staggered down the street, trying to wrap my mind around the concept that God does exist and that He had actually answered my two prayers.

"This changes everything," I thought. "I wonder what God's purpose for my life is, or if there is a purpose for life?"

Bargaining With God

I still continued to drink and do drugs for the next little while but observed that neither of these activities produced any inner peace in me. I finally concluded that I had given them a more-than-adequate try and did not find lasting peace in my life as a result of doing them. For this reason, I made the decision to search elsewhere for peace. I stopped drinking and doing drugs in one day.

Within the next month or so, I received my orders for Vietnam as an admin specialist. That night I prayed, "God, I will really believe in You, if You will just get me out of going to Vietnam."

God didn't answer my prayer. I learned why later. You see, God had already proven to me that He exists by answering two impossible prayers for me. He did not need to prove Himself to me again. I had already been convinced that God was real.

Second, that prayer was an attempt to manipulate God, not to worship Him; and God will never allow Himself to be manipulated! "I'll worship You as God, *if…*" is conditional worship, which is unacceptable for anyone who already believes in God.

Reporting to Vietnam

I arrived in DaNang, Vietnam, in April 1970, assigned to the 617th Military Airlift Support Squadron. We were located on the flight line of DaNang Air Base. Because DaNang was such a strategic air field, it was targeted regularly by rocket attacks from the Viet Cong.

I was terrified to go into that war zone. On the twenty-two-hour flight between California and DaNang, I found myself doing a lot of praying because of my desperation.

"Oh God," I cried, "I am terrified to die! I am also scared for other people to die around me. Why did you have to send me into this war zone? Can you *please* do something to protect us while I'm there?"

On that flight to Vietnam, I also had time to reflect on all the steps I had been through to try to discover who Shamblin Stone is and find some peace in my life.

"Maybe," I concluded, "I should try again to be a Christian. I may not have given it a good enough try, since I had previously lived a double life as a Christian."

"That's it!" I decided, "When I get to DaNang, I will be the best Christian anyone has ever seen." After all, this was the perfect opportunity to reinvent myself, because nobody would know what I had been like before.

For three days, I walked around DaNang with a Bible under my arm, telling everyone I was a Christian and that they should be a Christian too. I was really determined this time to make being a Christian work.

On the third day, I came into our squadron's day room after my duty-day was over. The day room was the only place in our barracks with an air conditioner. After work, the soldiers crowded in to watch reruns on an old black-and-white TV. The only channel we got was the Armed Forces Television Network.

I sat down beside a quiet guy, who was my target that day to witness Christianity to. "Hey," I leaned over to engage him in conversation, "Are you a Christian?"

"No!" came the quick response.

"Well, you ought to be!" I said to him.

"I'll think about it," he politely said to me, then went back to watching television.

Another soldier sitting in front of us whirled around and sharply addressed me, "Why don't you just shut up! Everybody knows you are nothing but a phony!"

He was right. I didn't have a clue what a true Christian was. Humiliated, I went to my room with a great sense of emptiness and despair. "Now who am I going to be?" I asked myself. I had no idea who Shamblin Stone was, and that day I lost all hope that I would ever find out.

"If only I had not convinced myself that drugs and alcohol offer no lasting peace," I scolded myself. Now I had nothing to dull the pain of being in that war zone. On top of this, I slept very little at night for fear I would wake up dead from a rocket attack.

All these factors contributed to the darkest depression I had ever known, which gave birth to my justification of suicidal thoughts all day, every day for the next two months.

Don Elliott

In the meantime, a young man named Don Elliott had arrived, assigned to our squadron. He was strange. Don was the only one of us who lived in peace in the middle of that war zone. He was always the last one down to the bunker when we were under rocket attacks. We would all be crouched down near the concrete walls when Don would come strolling down the stairs whistling or singing something like, "'Tis so sweet to trust in Jesus…"

Don Elliott in Vietnam in 1970

This would make our first sergeant very angry. "You're supposed to run down here, Elliot," he would shout. "Don't you know you could get killed out there?!"

"Of course," Don responded, always with a smile. "But my life is in the hands of Jesus. He will protect me! But if I do die, 'to be absent from the body is to be present with the Lord!'"

None of us had ever seen such insane peace before. "Could this guy be real?" we wondered. Among the soldiers in our squadron, there was a real buzz about Don. Several of the guys began to plot against him.

"We broke Stone of his religion in three days," one of the guys boasted. "Surely we can break 'Mr.' Elliott within the first two weeks!" this arrogant young airman proposed.

A couple of evenings later, they tried to do just that. When I was returning to my barrack's room after chow, I saw about fifteen guys standing outside Don's door, looking inside his room. I heard yelling and screaming coming from the room. When I got close enough, I noticed that two or three guys, who had previously declared they were atheists, were in the room with Don. They were arguing passionately why there is no God, firing questions at Don, yet not giving him a chance to answer. Frustrated and overwhelmed, Don began to weep.

"Well, look at the baby," one mocked. "He's crying!"

"I can't answer your questions," Don wept, "about why there is suffering and war in the world and why good people die. All I know is Jesus really loves you; and no matter what you do to me, I will love you too!"

To that statement, all three of Don's tormenters were speechless. After a long, awkward, silent pause, they stormed out of the room, unable to handle that kind of love. Nobody dared question Don's faith after that. Everyone knew it was genuine, although nobody could understand it. As for me, I just tried to avoid him completely. But God had different plans.

Daily Devotions

Don worked on the flight line, refueling airplanes all day. My office was a half block away from the flight line. Every morning on his way to the tarmac, Don would stop in and say hi. I wouldn't have minded it if that was all he did.

"I just wanted to share a scripture with you that I read in my devotions this morning," Don would always add. Then he would read the short scripture, look up with a smile, and say something like, "Didn't that just bless you?"

At first, I was polite to him, but after this continued day in and day out, I began to get really rude to him. "No!" I would raise my voice. "Get out of my office!" Don didn't stop coming every morning, reading the Bible to me, and he always had a smile, no matter how rude I was to him.

How I Committed Suicide

After a couple of months in country, my suicidal thoughts got the best of me. One night I sat in my room weeping uncontrollably. I decided that would be the night I would kill myself. All I had to do was figure out the best way to do it. The last thing I wanted was to fail at suicide. I had to figure out the best way to do it before anybody found out and tried to stop me.

"I could slit my wrist," I thought, "but that would hurt. Besides, how long would it take me to bleed to death?" I wondered. I figured it could take quite a while, and I didn't want a slow, painful death. Whatever I did would have to be quick and painless.

"I could take a bottle of pills," I thought. "That would be painless." There was only one problem—I didn't have a bottle of pills, and I didn't know where to get one at that time of night. Besides, I had heard so many stories where someone tried to kill himself with pills and he was always found before he died. I did not want to run the risk of that happening, so pills were out.

"If only I could get my hands on a gun," I thought. "That would be quick, and nobody could stop me." We had M16s assigned to us, but they were all locked up. "There is no way to get one," I realized, as I sat in my room crying.

I was at a loss. I wanted to kill myself, but I couldn't figure out how. That realization caused me to weep even harder.

Suddenly there was a loud knock at my door. I panicked. I didn't want anyone to see me crying. They might suspect something.

"Just a minute," I called out, wiping the tears from my face with my bare hands, trying to stop myself from crying. I couldn't take a long time getting to the door. Whomever it was, I couldn't let them suspect anything was wrong. Sniffing and wiping my nose, I opened my door.

There he stood, "Mr. Smiley," "Mr. Peace-in-a-war-zone."

"Hi," Don said, all cheerful-like.

"What are you doing here?" I said through clenched teeth.

"Well, Shamblin," Don began, "I was just down in my room asleep, and God woke me up. I felt like he was telling me you needed to talk to me."

With that, I began to weep again.

"What should I do?" I thought to myself. "He's seen me crying. My door is open. That means other people could see me crying too."

Without much thought, I reached out and grabbed Don's arm, yanked him into my room, and locked the door behind him. Still crying, I turned away from Don to try to figure out what I was going to do now.

"What's wrong?" Don asked.

"Nothing!" I snapped at him.

"Well, something's got to be wrong; otherwise you wouldn't be crying like this," Don persisted.

I was angry at the way Don had ruined my plans; I whirled around, and said deliberately through tears, "Well, if you must know, I was just sitting here trying to figure out how to kill myself!"

"You're going to kill yourself?" Don questioned intently.

"YES!" I barked.

"Well, praise God!" Don said excitedly. "That's the best news I've ever heard!"

With that, I stopped crying immediately. "What?" I yelled.

"How are you going to do it?" Don leaned in toward me.

"I don't know!" I screamed. "I'm just trying to figure that out."

"Can I tell you a good way?" Don smiled.

"Maybe this guy is crazy after all," I thought. "But if he's crazy, he might just have a good way to commit suicide. So, why not listen to him," I reasoned.

"Ok, how can I kill myself?" I asked, sarcastically.

"Well," Don said, unbuttoning the pocket on his fatigue shirt and pulling out his pocket New Testament, "rather than me tell you, I'm going to let Jesus tell you."

He turned to this passage of scripture and began to read.

> *For whosoever will save his life shall lose it. . . Matthew 16:25a KJV*

Pausing there, he looked up at me and asked, "Have you been trying to find your life?"

I thought back to all the attempts I had made to find out who Shamblin Stone is. "Yes," I answered. "How did you know?"

"Because you are about to lose it," he said calmly. "Let me read the rest of this scripture."

> *. . . and whosoever will lose his life for **My** sake shall find it. Matthew 16:25b KJV, emphasis added*

"If you want to kill yourself," he raised his open New Testament toward me, "do it this way! Give your life to Jesus, and you will find out what life is all about."

In that moment, I realized that being a Christian didn't have anything to do with what I did but with who was in charge of my life. I understood this concept for the first time by a supernatural revelation from the Holy Spirit.

I then began to weep once again. "God, I've made a mess of my life!" I prayed out loud. "I don't know why You would want it. But if You do, I give my life to You, Jesus! It's Yours!"

At that moment, an overwhelming sense of peace enveloped me. I had never known peace before in my life. Often, I had wondered what peace felt like—now I knew.

My first thoughts were that I had successfully killed myself in an easy, painless way. I was no longer in charge of my life, and it felt good! I had given my life to Jesus, and He had accepted it. He took my life, because I gave it to Him! Now Shamblin Stone was dead! Wow! What a concept! I am a dead man!

A few months later, I came across this scripture, which helped me understand what happened to me.

> *I am crucified with Christ, nevertheless I live. Yet not I, but Christ who lives in me. And the life I now live, I live by the faith of the Son of God Who loves me, and gave Himself for me. Galatians 2:20 KJV*

When you look at me, it appears like I am alive. But it is not me who lives—it is Jesus Christ who lives in me, living His life through me, because I gave up my life to Him.

Don's Sacrifice

I was the only convert Don had in DaNang. Because of that, Don spent many hours discipling me in the Word and in being led by the Spirit of God. I came to believe that I was the primary reason God sent him to DaNang.

DaNang was Don's second tour of duty in Vietnam in two and a half years. He had just met the love of his life before he got orders for Vietnam the first time. They corresponded for that year, and when Don arrived back in the United States, they began to make plans to get married in about six months.

Shamblin and Don in Vietnam, 1970 (Notice Don's pocket New Testament)

However, God began to lead Don that he needed to volunteer to go back to Vietnam for a second one-year tour of duty. As I understand it, Don's commander and his doctor tried their best to talk Don out of going back to Vietnam so soon, but Don was convinced he had heard from God and was determined to go. Don and his wife Coleen were married just a week before he was on the plane back to Vietnam, knowing they would spend another year apart.

I am so thankful God put Don right where he was when I needed him, and I am so very glad Don knew how to be led by the Spirit! I can never repay Don and Coleen's sacrifice so I would be rescued!

Although Don came to DaNang more than two months after I did,  mysteriously, just a few days after I returned stateside, Don received orders to return to the United States immediately as well. Nobody had ever heard of that much time being shaved off of a one-year tour and that quickly. With me gone, I believe Don's work in DaNang was finished. So, God let him return home to his wife. At least, that's my theory.

Don, Coleen, & Shamblin
reunited 1994

An Amazing Miracle

After I had been in Vietnam about six months, a Christian Sargent who was getting ready to return home was reflecting on his year there in DaNang.

"You know, it's crazy," he began. "When I first got here, people were being killed every week from rocket attacks. But it's been a good six months since anyone has been killed on this base from a rocket."

"I believe I know why," Frank, a fellow Christian spoke up. "My wife is part of a prayer group in our church back home, and they have been praying since I got here that no one would be killed on this base."

"Well, praise the Lord," the sergeant responded. "Tell her to keep praying!"

After I returned to my barracks room that day, I felt the Lord reminded me of that conversation.

"Frank has only been in country four months," I remembered. "Why, then, have there been no deaths on this base for six months?" I wondered.

At that moment, I remembered the prayer I prayed in the plane on the way to Vietnam. "Who am I," my eyes filled with tears, "that God would answer my prayer like this?" Right then, God flooded me with His peace and joy, as I was reassured of His love for me!

Rocket Duds

It's not that we did not have as many rocket attacks as before; it's just that the rockets that could have caused death were all duds. One rocket came through the roof of a barracks and landed in the middle of a card table where four or five soldiers were playing cards. None of them were physically hurt, yet I heard they were sent home early because of the trauma of that event.

One of the guys in our squadron was walking back to the barracks one evening when a rocket landed about five feet away from him, according to his report. It hit in the middle of the street. The bomb squad found the nose of the rocket was buried two and a half feet into the asphalt and ground. When I saw the rocket a couple hours later, about five-and-a-half feet of it was sticking out of the street. These rockets were almost a foot in diameter, and the rockets' steel cylinders were about two inches thick. The inside of the rocket was full of explosives, and when the trigger on the nose of the rocket was tripped, the explosives in the rocket would shred the steel casing into small, razor-sharp pieces of shrapnel. These flying shrapnel could kill someone more than a block away.

C-130 Pilot Spared

Here's a picture of a C-130 plane parked about thirty yards away from my office. The only thing between this plane and my office was what is called a "blast fence" made from two-by-twelves. The fence was about eight feet tall. A blast fence is meant to protect the buildings and people from the

This C130 took a direct hit with a Viet Cong rocket

jet engines' exhaust when planes are pulling away from their parking spot. The pilot of this plane was planning to spend the night in it when he suddenly got the urge to go into my building and get a drink before going to sleep. He had just walked around the blast fence when his plane took a direct hit with a rocket. No shrapnel hit him, because the blast fence protected him.

The Blast Fence 15 yards away from the building I worked in on the DaNang flight line

Fuel Dump Hit

The jet engine fuel was stored in huge nylon or canvas bladders, which were on the tarmac, surrounded by eight-foot-high asphalt, rectangular bowls. These were called fuel dumps. They were designed like this so in the case that the bladders ruptured, the fuel would not run all over the runway.

A DaNang Flight-line Fuel Dump

The next picture, which I took from my barracks room doorway at about 2:10 a.m., is of a fuel dump. My barracks was one short block from the flight line. A rocket had hit the fuel dump, and flames were about 250 feet high. It was so hot we could feel the heat from our barracks. The jet engine fuel fire is lighting up the Pan American

Airlines plane parked near the fuel dump. It was scheduled to load at

DaNang Air Field Fuel Dump Fire

2:00 a.m., but for some reason the pilot made the decision not to load the plane till about 2:30 a.m. This decision probably saved the lives of the soldiers who would have been lined up outside the plane waiting to board.

The lighted sign in the lower left-hand corner of the picture identifies this sign at the entrance of the 15th Aerial Port waiting area, one block from my barracks. You can make out the straight, top edge of that terminal building going over

Lighted Sign at the Main Entrance of the DaNang Air Port

to about the middle of the fire. The plane is about a block away from the airport terminal building.

I have many more stories of lives saved during the year I was in Vietnam. The week after Don and I left Vietnam, people started dying every week at DaNang from rocket attacks. As far as I know, this continued until the end of the war.

Reflecting on the Journey

As I look back over the journey God has taken me on since Vietnam, I find that Jesus has kept His word to me. He also has answered many of my prayers—resulting in major miracles at the level of what I have just described.

Because I gave my life to Jesus, He has in turn taught me the true purpose of life. In addition to this, I thank God that, after all these years, I still have God's peace in my life!

> *Peace I leave with you, my peace I give unto you: not as the world giveth, give I unto you. Let not your heart be troubled, neither let it be afraid. John 14:27 KJV*

Chapter 1

The Purpose of Life

The Age-Old Question

I entered the United States Air Force on December 31, 1968. We rang in the New Year standing at attention in the hallway of our barracks, listening to our training instructor (TI) yell in our faces till 2:00 a.m. Basic training was quite the experience. I wondered more than once if I had made the right decision by joining the military.

One day our TI marched us to the base theater to see a movie. It was part of our basic training, so the film was not produced in Hollywood. It was a US Armed Forces' production.

The lights in the theater went dim, and the movie started with the title "Why Are We Here?" Immediately I sat up in my chair, expecting to get some answers as to why I joined the air force. I needed a real pep talk at that time about how important it is for us to serve our country.

However, I was shocked to find out that this movie was an overview of the different philosophical opinions throughout history addressing the age-old question of the purpose or meaning of human life. None of the philosophers highlighted in the movie agreed with each other, so the movie came to no conclusions as to what the purpose of life is.

As I walked away from the theater that day, I felt empty. For the first time in my life, I felt there was no reason for me to live. For two days, I considered suicide; then the depression eased up, and I stopped thinking about that movie. However, this hopeless desperation is what finally matured in me in DaNang, Vietnam, and caused me to give up my own life and turn it over to Jesus.

Looking back on that movie, I can see that it completely lacked Judeo-Christian influence. No wonder it depressed me so much. Apart from Jesus, there is no real hope in this world.

A few years later, when I was attending college, I found myself in a required philosophy course. It was an in-depth study of what that armed forces movie covered. Again, I noticed the total absence of Judeo-Christian influences, even though I was attending a Christian university.

Where Should We Look for Answers?

Opinions about this very important question are as varied and extreme as they possibly can be. Since the most-brilliant minds of history have debated this issue and have not come to a consensus, where, then, are we to turn to find the answer to this all-important question? What indeed is the purpose of our life? What were we created to be or to do?

To find answers to these perplexing questions, we must go to the Creator of life Himself. Fortunately, He has written a best-selling book on this very subject.

Creation, Not Evolution

I realize that many people in the world today do not believe in a creator but hold to the evolution explanation of the universe's origin. A reason for this is because it has been not acceptable to teach the possibility of intelligent design of the physical universe in all our publicly accredited education institutions for many years. Because of this, we have had several generations grow up without the fundamental knowledge of God as the Creator.

It is not my intention to present you with the scientific evidence for believing in creation and a Creator in this book. There are many resources you can turn to for this proof. One such resource is a DVD distributed by Jeremiah Films entitled *The Evolution Conspiracy*. You can order this DVD online at www.jeremiahfilms.com or by calling 800-828-2290. It is well worth the money you will spend for it.

What Does Creation Have to Do with Worship?

Psalms 100 is a short chapter by Bible standards, but it reveals to us some of the most important revelations concerning worship in the entire Bible. As a student of worship, you should read it often, even memorize it. This short chapter is pivotal to the understanding of worship. Take time to read it now. Here it is in the old King James Version of the Bible.

> *Make a joyful noise unto the LORD, all ye lands. Serve the LORD with gladness: come before his presence with singing. Know ye that the LORD he is God: it is he that hath made us, and not we ourselves; we are his people, and the sheep of his pasture. Enter into his gates with thanksgiving, and into his courts with praise: be thankful unto him, and bless his name. For the LORD is good; his mercy is everlasting; and his truth endureth to all generations. Psalms 100:1–5 KJV*

Here is a brief outline of these five verses.

➢ Our praise should be joyful and loud.
➢ God's vision is for nations to glorify Him.
➢ Our service to God is our worship of God.
➢ We should worship the Lord with gladness, not out of duty.
➢ God's manifested presence is the result of our praise.[1]
➢ Our corporate worship should be done primarily with singing.
➢ We worship from the knowledge of who God is and what He does.
➢ Praise starts with a thankful attitude.
➢ Praise is perpetuated by the revelation of God's character.

This is just a quick overview outline of this chapter. There are multiple layers of truth here, some of which will be discussed later in

---

[1] Ps 22:3.

this book and in the next two books of this series. What I want to look at right now in Psalms 100 is what will answer the question I asked, "What does creation have to do with worship?" The answer is found in the first part of verse three.

> *Know ye that the LORD he is God: it is he that hath made*
> *us, and not we ourselves; Psalms 100:3a KJV*

The context of Psalms 100 is praise, and God is telling us here in this scripture that every worshiper must worship God from the knowledge that God made us. Evolution teaches us that mankind created ourselves through the process of natural selection. Therefore, it is not Biblical worship to praise God while believing in evolution. This is also taught in Romans 1. Creation is a cardinal truth of Christianity, which cannot be compromised; just like the virgin birth of Jesus cannot be compromised.

If you doubt God's Word, you doubt God Himself! God even places His Word as more important than His name, which is above every other name.

> *I will worship toward thy holy temple, and praise thy name*
> *for thy lovingkindness and for thy truth: for thou hast*
> *magnified thy word above all thy name. Psalms 138:2 KJV*

The Word Is the Revelation of God to Man

Since the Creator Himself has authored a best-selling book on the very subject of why He created the universe, He has made it very easy for us to find out the answers to our questions about why He created us. His book is the Holy Bible.

The Bible, we believe, is God-inspired. In other words, it was written by God the Holy Spirit through men who yielded themselves to God's Spirit, so He could write through them.

> *For no prophecy recorded in scripture was ever thought*
> *up by the prophet himself. It was the Holy Spirit within*

these godly men who gave them true messages from God.
2 Peter 1:20 Living

Because of this, we believe that the Holy Spirit completely inspired the original text of the Holy scriptures. Every dotting of an "i" or crossing of a "t" was inspired by God Himself. Therefore, the scripture in its original state is infallible.

> *I tell you the truth, until heaven and earth disappear, not the smallest letter, not the least stroke of a pen, will by any means disappear from the Law until everything is accomplished. Matthew 5:18 NIV*

As in this scripture we just read, it was common to refer to the Bible as the "Law." Here is another reference to the Bible as the "Word."

> *Study to show thyself approved unto God, a workman that needeth not to be ashamed, rightly dividing the **word** of truth. 2 Tim 2:15 KJV, emphasis added*

God is as true as His word. To doubt God's word is to doubt God Himself. If you believe in God, you *must* believe in His Word. You cannot separate God from His word, the Bible!

The "Word" in these next scriptures refers to a person. That person is Jesus, who is the only "begotten" son of God. The rest of us are adopted into God's family when we make Jesus our Lord.

> *In the beginning was the Word, and the Word was with God, and the Word was God. The same was in the beginning with God. All things were made by Him; and without Him was not anything made that was made. In Him was life; and the life was the light of men. And the light shineth in darkness; and the darkness comprehended it not. John 1:1–5 KJV*
>
> *And the Word was made flesh, and dwelt among us, (and we beheld His glory, the glory as of the only begotten of the Father,) full of grace and truth. John 1:14 KJV*

Jesus was not just a prophet or a good teacher. Jesus was God revealing Himself to His creation. God revealed Himself to us in His written Word, the Bible, and in His living Word, Jesus. Jesus is the revelation of God to mankind come to earth in the flesh.

> *And without controversy great is the mystery of godliness:*
> *God was manifest in the flesh, justified in the Spirit, seen*
> *of angels, preached unto the Gentiles, believed on in the*
> *world, received up into glory. 1 Timothy 3:16 KJV*

Jesus is God come in the flesh. He was totally God while here on earth.

> *For in Him dwells all the fullness of the Godhead bodily;*
> *Colossians 2:9 NKJV*

The written Word of God is also the revelation of Jesus the Word. Listen to the way Jesus said this when He walked on this earth in the flesh.

> *Search the scriptures; for in them ye think ye have eternal*
> *life: and they are they which testify of me. John 5:39 KJV*

The written Word of God and the Word come in the flesh both reveal Jesus to us, and Jesus is God come to earth in the flesh!

The Importance of Reading the Bible and Praying

When I enrolled in my first college writing class, my teacher, Elsie Platt, told us that by the time she had read our third writing assignment, she would know more about us than some of us knew about ourselves. She told us that when we write, no matter what subject we write about, we reveal ourselves to the reader.

That's what God does in His written word, the Bible, and in Jesus the living Word. Therefore, the Word is God's revelation of Himself to mankind.

Do you want to know God? If so, you must do two things. First, you must read what He has written to you. Read some of the Bible every day. However, it is not enough to read the Bible once and never read it again.

The Bible was written by God. Therefore, every time you read it, you will learn something new. The Bible has multiple layers of truth, unlike books written by ordinary men and women.

Second, you must spend time daily in conversation with Jesus. We call this type of conversation between mankind and God "prayer." However, a true conversation is one where each person takes their turn talking, and listening. Prayer is talking to God, and also listening to God. If you are a Christian, Jesus wants to talk to you every day.

You may feel that you cannot hear God's voice. However, Jesus told us that we all can learn to recognize His voice.

> *My sheep hear my voice, and I know them, and they follow me: John 10:27 KJV*

If you cannot hear God's voice, it is not because He is not talking to you. It is simply because you have not yet learned to recognize His voice speaking with your spirit. To grow accustomed to Jesus' voice, read the Bible more. The Bible is the way God speaks. The more time you spend reading the Bible, the more you will learn to recognize Jesus' voice when He speaks to you directly.

In review, these are the two primary ways God has chosen to reveal Himself to men—the Bible and Jesus. In the Bible, you will also learn of many secondary ways that God uses to reveal himself, like writing on walls, talking through donkeys, and sending fire down from heaven, etc.

Jesus, the Word, Is the Creator of All that exists

The first thing we learn about God in the Bible is that He is a creator.

> *In the beginning God created. . . Genesis 1:1 KJV*

How God created is very important to note at this time. Creation occurred by the Word of God. Therefore, all we know in this natural world—animal, vegetable, and mineral—was created by the Word of God. Here is an overview (emphasis added) of the creation account in

Genesis from the viewpoint of God speaking everything into existence by His Word.

> And **God said**, *Let there be light. . . Genesis 1:3 KJV*
>
> And **God said**, *Let there be a firmament. . . Genesis 1:6 KJV*
>
> And **God said**, *Let the waters. . . Genesis 1:9 KJV*
>
> And **God said**, *Let the earth bring forth grass. . . Genesis 1:11 KJV*
>
> And **God said**, *Let there be lights. . . Genesis 1:14 KJV*
>
> And **God said**, *Let the waters bring forth abundantly. . . Genesis 1:20 KJV*
>
> And **God said**, *Let the earth bring forth the living creature. . . Genesis 1:24 KJV*
>
> And **God said**, *Let us make man. . . Genesis 1:26 KJV*

As we have learned before, Jesus *is* the Word or the revelation of God. Therefore, Jesus is the creator of all that exists. God created everything by His own Word, and the living Word of God is Jesus.

> *All things were made by Him; and without Him was not anything made that was made. John 1:3 KJV*

The Two Realms of Creation

By reading the Bible, we learn that there are two coexisting realms of God's creation. Not only did Jesus create everything in the universe, which is the natural realm, but He also created the entire spiritual realm. I first introduced this to you in the book *Biblical Worship*, published by Westbow Press in 2012. Here is a brief review of that study for those of you who have not read that book.

> *In whom we have redemption through his blood, even the forgiveness of sins: Who is the image of the invisible God, the firstborn of every creature: For by him were all things created, that are in heaven, and that are in earth, visible and invisible, whether they be thrones, or dominions,*

*or principalities, or powers: all things were created by
Him. . . Colossians 1:14–16 KJV*

The first sentence of this scripture talks about "redemption through
His blood," and the Bible teaches us that the one who shed His blood
to redeem mankind was Jesus. This identifies for us without any doubt
who is being talked about here.

This scripture then tells us that Jesus created two realms to exist side
by side. The one is the natural realm; the second is the spiritual realm.
Notice in this scripture how each of these two realms relate to Jesus as
their creator. The word "Creature" in this scripture refers to the physical
body of mankind, like Jesus had while He lived on earth. Jesus did not
take on a physical body until many years into the existence of the natural
realm, even though He created it. Therefore, since Jesus existed before
any other man, He is called "the firstborn of every creature."

In other places in the Bible, this word "Creature" can also refer to
the other living "creatures" God caused to inhabit the earth (natural
realm). Without our spirit and soul, mankind is simply another of earth's
creatures.

Now look at the lists of things God created (outlined in this scripture)
for each of these two realms.

The Two Different Realms of Creation in Colossians 1:14-16

The Spiritual Realm	The Natural Realm
Jesus, the image of the invisible God	Jesus, the firstborn of every creature
Heaven	Earth
Invisible	Visible
Principalities	Thrones
Powers	Dominions

Table I

We understand from Ephesians 6 that principalities and powers are part of the hierarchy of the demonic kingdom, which exists in the spiritual realm. Therefore, God created all beings, even the ones who rebelled against Him and were banished from heaven to the earth.

Another way of saying "thrones and dominions" is to say "governments and countries." After all, Canada is called a dominion.

From this scripture, we conclude that Jesus is the creator of everything that exists, both in the natural realm and the spiritual realm.

> *All things were made by Him; and without Him was not anything made that was made. John 1:3 KJV*

Both the natural realm and the spiritual realm are coexisting together in the same physical location. Mankind is both spiritual and natural at the same time. Angels are spirit beings, which have the capability to take on the form of natural things. In Psalms 104:4, we learn that God has given His ministering angels the ability to appear in the natural realm as fire, which does not consume. In the book of Hebrews, we learn that God has also given the angels the ability to appear as a human being.

> *Be not forgetful to entertain strangers: for thereby some have entertained angels unawares. Hebrews 13:2 KJV*

Let me share one more point about angels at this time. This helps us understand the difference between mankind and angels. The purpose of angels' lives is defined in this scripture.

> *But to which of the angels said he at any time, Sit on my right hand, until I make thine enemies thy footstool? Are they not all ministering spirits, sent forth to minister for them who shall be heirs of salvation? Hebrews 1:13–14 KJV*

The human race is the only part of God's creation that qualifies for salvation. Because of Adam and Eve's sin, God came into our physical world and paid the price of His own blood to redeem us. A multitude of angels sinned, but they were not created in the image of God; they were not destined to be the children of God. When angels sinned, God created a lake of fire to punish them. When mankind sinned, God made a way for us to be forgiven.

The declared purpose of all angels is "to minister for them who shall be heirs of salvation."

The Creator's Pleasure

Every creation or invention is made with a specific purpose in mind. Alexander Graham Bell needed to be able to communicate with his servant when the two were not in the same room. Thomas Edison wanted to illuminate a room without burning candles or oil lamps. He used the power of electricity to supply what was needed for his light bulb to work, and eventually he replaced the open flame with the light bulb as the preferred source of light. Henry Ford wanted to be able to travel from one place to another without having to hitch up the horse, so he invented (or created) the automobile.

Each of these inventions was designed with a specific purpose in mind. When the inventions functioned the way their creators hoped they would, that brought pleasure to their creators. The difference between these inventors and Jesus is that Jesus created everything out of nothing. These men had to use the raw materials that God created to form their inventions.

Since Jesus existed as God from before the foundations of the world, the person for whom He created everything could only be Himself. Let's read this scripture again, this time in its entirety.

> *For by Him were all things created, that are in heaven, and that are in earth, visible and invisible, whether they be thrones, or dominions, or principalities, or powers: all things were created by Him, and for Him: And He is before all things, and by Him all things consist. Colossians 1:16–17 KJV, emphasis added*

All of creation was created *by* Jesus (who is God) and *for* Jesus to bring Him pleasure.

> *Thou art worthy, O Lord, to receive glory and honor and power: for Thou hast created all things, and for Thy **pleasure** they are and were created. Revelation 4:11 KJV, emphasis added*

The Balance of Nature Is Not the Purpose of Life

God did not create His creations to simply perpetuate themselves, void of Him. To believe that the only purpose of life is primarily to "be fruitful and multiply"[2] is to say that God has set in motion a plan where man lives for man's sake, and everything else exists to perpetuate all of life. Such a worldly philosophy was rebuked sharply by Paul in 1 Corinthians 6. In this scripture, Paul first stated this worldly philosophy in its simplest form and then he devastated it by the truth.

> *Meats for the belly, and the belly for meats: but God shall destroy both it and them. Now the body is not for fornication, but for the Lord; and the Lord for the body. 1 Corinthians 6:13 KJV*

This seemingly noble, worldly philosophy is based on mankind's concept of the balance of nature. Let me say it this way: "Cows, chickens, turkeys, game, plus grains, fruits, and vegetables exist to be food for the human race, and mankind exists for the purpose of eating this food." For a natural man, this is a reasonably commendable philosophy, but it is far beneath what God intended for all of life.

This philosophy is actually the basic premise on which many philosophical writers have built their theories. After all, frogs keep down the fly population, don't they? So, the flies must have been created for the frogs to have something to eat. And the frogs were created to keep down

---

[2] Gen. 1:28 (King James Version)

the fly population, right? Wrong! Whereas God established a balance in nature, that balance is not His purpose for His creation.

This is nothing more than a fatalistic idealism, which has been applied to many things. For instance, we have seen this philosophy adapted to all mankind's basic needs.

Natural Philosophy of Life

Meats for the belly/body	And the belly/body for meats
Sleep for the body	And the body for sleep
Sex for the body	And the body for sex
Clothes for the body	And the body for clothes
Shelter for the body	And the body for shelter

Table II

It was Adam and Eve's sin that caused the last two items to be added to this list of basic needs. As we review history, we see that society's attitude toward these has developed according to this basic philosophy, which Paul quoted. We have even made it a joke, which is declared from lips and bumper stickers alike, that the purpose of our existence is to obtain clothing and items for our dwellings, etc. Yes, we have boldly declared our philosophy of life with the bumper sticker that reads "Born to Shop."

I also need to add two more items to this list of basic human needs—transportation and work.

For thousands of years, man had no transportation apart from using the animals God created. However, since the invention of the various types of engines, transportation has been provided by the witty inventions of mankind. Of course, we know that God is the one who gives mankind the ideas and abilities to create these inventions. Nothing advances apart from God.

> It is God's privilege to conceal things, and the king's privilege to discover and invent. Proverbs 25:2 Living

Adult Humans' Basic Needs

Here is the list of seven fundamental basic needs of mankind in the order of their importance to the average human adult.

1. Food and drink
2. Sleep and rest
3. Clothing
4. Shelter
5. Purpose or work
6. Sexual activity and parenting
7. Transportation or mobility

Let's look at a couple of these basic needs briefly in light of the popular worldly philosophy that Paul quoted in 1 Corinthians 6:13.

Food and Drink

It is true that our bodies are designed to take in and process food and drink—and by it sustain life—yet this hardly could be considered our purpose for existence.

Sleep and Rest

It is also true that without sleep our bodies and brains cease to function properly; yet, it is wrong for us to say that the purpose of our life is to sleep and that sleep was created so that our body would have sleep as our purpose.

We could examine every one of our basic needs in this same way and come up with the same conclusion for each one. When we read further in 1 Corinthians 6:13, we hear Paul argue that we are leaving out one important fact.

> . . . but God shall destroy both it and them. . . 1 Corinthians
> 6:13 KJV

Both the food supply and our bodies are only temporary. One day our bodies, as we know them, will be done away with. We will not have the basic needs we now have; because, for Christians, we will have a new body, fashioned like the Lord's glorified body.

> *But our citizenship is in heaven. And we eagerly await a Savior from there, the Lord Jesus Christ, Who, by the power that enables Him to bring everything under His control, will transform our lowly bodies so that they will be like His glorious body. Philippians 3:20–21NIV*

So, what is Jesus' glorified body like since He was resurrected from the dead? The Bible tells us that Jesus ate and processed food, but his body was no longer bound by the common laws of physics of this world. For starters, He could appear and disappear at will.

> *And it came to pass, as he sat at meat with them, he took bread, and blessed it, and brake, and gave to them. And their eyes were opened, and they knew him; and he vanished out of their sight. Luke 24:30–31 KJV*

Sexual Activity

After Paul reminded the Corinthians that our bodies and this world are temporary, he then addressed humans' sex drive. Now, it is true that God gave sexual intercourse between a man and a woman to the human race and that it plays a very important role in marital relationships and the procreation of human life. But, Paul says, you've missed the point. The body was not made for sexual pleasures, unless it is in the context of marriage. Yet, even then, sex is not the purpose for which our bodies were created. Our bodies were created for the Lord, to give Him pleasure. Our bodies were not created for ourselves, to give us pleasure. And if we insist on carrying this simple, carnal, philosophical equation over into Godly matters, then Paul says, ". . . and the Lord for the body."

This, of course, does not mean that Paul is saying that Jesus is a created being, created only for the purpose of deriving pleasure from the bodies of the human race. Paul is simply showing that to apply spiritual truths to worldly concepts is impossible. The two do not mix. Since we, mankind, insist on thinking things out our own way, Paul—by that last statement—simply proves how ridiculous this entire philosophical premise is in the first place. However, the truth of the first half of the statement still remains. This truth can be summed up like this: Our body does not exist to have its needs satisfied—it exists for the Lord's satisfaction and pleasure. We will examine the specific ways our bodies are to bring God pleasure later in this book.

The Purpose of Life Is to Bring God Pleasure

We see that God did not create the natural realm for itself but for Himself to bring Him pleasure. Let's read that scripture again.

> *Thou art worthy, O Lord, to receive glory and honor and power: for Thou hast created all things, and for Thy **pleasure** they are and were created. Revelation 4:11 KJV, emphasis added*

The question we need to ask now is "Exactly how does God's creation bring Him pleasure?" To answer this, we need to start by understanding that, just like there are two different realms of creation, there are also two categories of God's Natural Creation. We divide them this way:

1. That which was created in the image and likeness of God—humanity
2. Everything else that God created in the natural realm

Study the chart below to understand what I am saying.

Understanding Creation

The Two Realms of Creation	
The spiritual realm	The natural realm

The Two Categories of Natural Creation	
Created in the image of God	Everything else

Table III

Free Will

One of the fundamental differences between the two categories of God's natural creation is free will, or the ability to choose our destiny. This was given only to the part of God's natural creation that was created in God's image. Nothing else in nature has a choice of how to function. God put within all other natural creation preprogrammed functions. In vegetation, some plants creep and spread out. Other plants grow tall. In animals, instincts are their preprogrammed behavior.

God has given all spiritual beings a free will. Lucifer is a spirit being, whom God created. He chose to rebel in heaven. Also, one-third of the angels decided to follow Lucifer when he rebelled. Here is what Lucifer said when he decided to rebel against God.

> *How art thou fallen from heaven, O Lucifer, son of the morning! How art thou cut down to the ground, which didst weaken the nations! For thou hast said in thine heart, **I will** ascend into heaven, **I will** exalt my throne above the stars of God: **I will** sit also upon the mount of the congregation, in the sides of the north: **I will** ascend above the heights of the clouds; **I will** be like the most High. Isaiah 14:12–14 KJV, emphasis added*

Lucifer chose to do what he did. Remember, Lucifer is an angel, and angels are spirit beings. All spirit beings have a free will.

Because men and women are spirit beings, we have a free will also. However, because we are fleshly beings as well, we struggle sometimes with making the correct choices.

Natural Creation Functioning as Designed

Remember, we said an invention or creation is designed and made with a specific purpose in mind. When that invention or creation functions the way it was designed to, it brings the inventor or creator pleasure.

Please read the creation account from the Bible in Genesis 1. As you read the scriptures, follow along with this chart. Start with Genesis 1:1.

The Days of Creation

Scripture	Day	What was Created	What God said
Genesis 1:4–5	first day	light	"it was good"
Genesis 1:8–10	second day	the firmament, dry land, seas	"it was good"
Genesis 1:12–13	third day	grass, herbs, trees	"it was good"
Genesis 1:14–19	fourth day	seasons, days, years, sun, moon, stars	"it was good"
Genesis 1:21–23	fifth day	whales, every sea creature and winged foul	"it was good"
Genesis 1:24–25	sixth day	creatures, cattle, creeping things, and beasts	"it was good," verse 25; "it was very good," verse 31
Genesis 1:26–31	sixth day	man—male and female	//////////

Table IV

Notice that on every day of creation God declared that what He had made was "good."

We can only imagine how excited the Wright brothers were when their airplane actually flew according to the way they designed it to fly. What all creators or inventors want is to see their creation actually functioning the way it was designed to function.

The *Theological Dictionary of the Old Testament* gives us the Hebrew word *tôb*[3] (pronounced *tōv*) for the English word "good" in these scriptures. Here is what this reference book has to say.

> *"The most common meaning of 'tôb' in the OT is utilitarian. From the perspective of the suitability of an object or person, the focus is on the functional aspect, as being in proper order or suited for the job. We are thus dealing with "goodness" for something.*

Let's put it into layman's terms. "Good" in this context actually means "functioning as designed." That means, when God stood back at the end of each day of creation and examined what He made that day, He saw that it was functioning the way He had designed it to. In other words, when God saw His creation was "good," it meant that He saw it was working. The pig was being a pig. The fish was being a fish; and the planets were being planets. By functioning the way God designed everything to function, God's creation was immediately showing forth His glory.

> *For since the creation of the world His invisible attributes are clearly seen, being understood by the things that are made, even His eternal power and Godhead, so that they are without excuse, Romans 1:20 NKJV*

For those of you who prefer using the *Vine's Bible Dictionary*,[4] it also goes to great lengths to explain the meaning of this word "good," which God used in the creation story. Both of these reference books indicate that the word "good" means far more in Hebrew than just "a sense of pleasure."

Vine's tells us that, when you use the word "good" in reference to

---

[3] Botterweck, G. Johannes, Helmer Ringgren, Heinz-Josef Fabry (Eds.), *Theological Dictionary of the Old Testament* (Vol. V) (D. E. Green, Trans.), 304. Grand Rapids: William B. Eerdmans Publishing Company, 1986.

[4] Vine, W. E., M.F. Unger, W. White Jr. *Vine's Complete Expository Dictionary of Old and New Testament Words*, accessed on February 3, 2017, http://www.ultimatebiblereferencelibrary.com/Vines_Expository_Dictionary.pdf.

God's creation, such as land or vegetation, it "suggests its potential of supporting life (Deuteronomy. 11:17). Thus the expression 'the good land' is a comment about not only its existing, but its potential, productivity."[5]

In other words, telling land or vegetation or natural creation of any kind that it is "good" is saying it is accomplishing what it was created to accomplish.

Noah Webster's *American Dictionary of the English Language*, published in 1828, gives this as the third definition to the word "good" and includes the following Bible reference.

> *3. Complete or sufficiently perfect in its kind; having the physical qualities best adapted to its design and use; opposed to bad, imperfect, corrupted, impaired. We say, good timber, good cloth, a good soil, a good color.*
> *"And God saw every thing that he had made, and behold, it was very good." Genesis 1:31.*[6]

Every time God created something, He looked very closely to make sure it was *tôb*. When God saw it was, He would "glory" in that part of His creation. In other words, not only does all of creation bring God pleasure and joy by functioning properly, but it also reveals God's greatness and glory to the angels and mankind.

> *The heavens declare the glory of God; the skies proclaim the work of His hands. Day after day pours forth speech; night after night displays knowledge. There is no speech or language where their voice is not heard. Their voice goes out into all the earth, their words to the ends of the world. Psalms 19:1–4 NIV, paraphrased*

The heavens are operating with clear precision, which declares to every spirit being God's glory. The way one day goes into another and night follows every day with such intricate timing speaks volumes

---

[5] Vine's Complete Expository Dictionary.
[6] Webster, N. American Dictionary of the English Language. (1828).

about God's glory and majesty. This speech of God's creation is heard throughout all the earth.

> *For since the creation of the world God's invisible qualities—His eternal power and divine nature—have been clearly seen, being understood from what has been made, so that men are without excuse. Romans 1:20 NIV*

God's creation functions wonderfully according to the way He designed it to function. This is the way creation declares the glory of Almighty God, by being *tôb*.

> *But ask now the beasts, and they shall teach thee; and the fowls of the air, and they shall tell thee: Or speak to the earth, and it shall teach thee: and the fishes of the sea shall declare unto thee. Who knoweth not in all these that the hand of the LORD hath wrought this? in whose hand is the soul of every living thing ("creature" in NIV), and the breath of all mankind. Job 12:7–10 KJV*

It is important that we point out the two categories of natural creation articulated in this last scripture as proof that God has divided His natural creation into these two categories.

> *...**every** living **thing** ("creature" in NIV), and the breath of all **mankind**. Job 12:10 KJV emphasis added*

Here is another scripture that separates God's natural creation into these two categories.

> *And God remembered **Noah**, and **every** living **thing**, and all the cattle that was with him in the ark: and God made a wind to pass over the earth, and the waters asswaged; Genesis 8:1 KJV, emphasis added*

Mankind is not a "thing" to God like the other creatures. We were made in God's image. God is not a thing—therefore, we are not things!

Here is a chart to show how these two scriptures validate the two categories of natural creation.

The Two Categories of Natural Creation

Scripture	Every Living Thing	Created in the Image of God
Job 12:10	every living "thing"	all mankind
Genesis 8:1	every living thing and cattle	Noah (family is implied, which is all mankind after the flood)

Table V

Let me summarize what I have been saying. The way natural creation brings pleasure to God is by functioning the way God designed it to function. God preprogrammed every living thing to function a certain way. However, mankind must choose to function the way we are designed in order to bring God pleasure.

Humanity Must Choose to Function as Designed

The only part of God's natural creations that God did not declare was *tôb* when He created it was the one created in His own image: mankind. Man did not, and does not, automatically function in the way he was designed to function. God honors mankind's free will and allows us the choice to function in the way He designed us or to choose not to function that way.

Genesis 1 tells us that God did not declare mankind to be good at the time He created us. Now, some Bible scholars believe that the phrase in Genesis 1:31, "... *behold, it was very good...*" refers to mankind. That simply is not true, and it is easily understood when we read the scripture in context.

> *And God said, Let Us make man in our image, after our likeness: and let them have dominion over the fish of the sea, and over the fowl of the air, and over the cattle, and*

over all the earth, and over every creeping thing that creepeth upon the earth. ²⁷ So God created man in His own image, in the image of God created He him; male and female created He them. ²⁸ And God blessed them, and God said unto them, Be fruitful, and multiply, and replenish the earth, and subdue it: and have dominion over the fish of the sea, and over the fowl of the air, and over every living thing that moveth upon the earth.

*²⁹ And God said, Behold, I have given you every herb bearing seed, which is upon the face of all the earth, and every tree, in the which is the fruit of a tree yielding seed; to you it shall be for meat. ³⁰ **And** to every beast of the earth, and to every fowl of the air, and to every thing that creepeth upon the earth, wherein there is life, I have given every green herb for meat: and it was so. ³¹ And God saw every **thing** that He had made, and, behold, it was very good. And the evening and the morning were the sixth day. Genesis 1:26–31 KJV*

Notice in verse 27, God created mankind. Then in verse 28, God blessed mankind. The next thing that took place was a teaching session about eating. God had to teach man this, but He preprogrammed it into all the other creatures as an instinct.

As the lesson unfolded in verse 29, God taught man that he would have to eat to sustain life. This shows that God created man with intelligence beyond any of His other created beings and that God wanted man to use his intelligence to advance and grow—which we have done. It also proves that mankind is the only part of God's natural creation with the gift of intelligent speech—the ability to communicate specific thoughts and feelings with beings of equal and higher intelligence.

As God was teaching man about what He had provided man to eat, He also made sure to point out that man would have to share some of this food supply with the other creatures that God had created and placed on the earth. It was at that moment that God's attention returned to the creatures He had just made that day, which prompted joy and pleasure for Him. That's when God welled up with pride over all He had made before making man on that sixth day, and that's why He joyfully declared that all that He had made before man was "very good" in verse 31.

At the time of creation, God never once declared mankind to be *tôb*. By this we understand that God created mankind to function in a specific purpose that mankind would not automatically function in, like the rest of God's creations do, because man is the only part of God's natural creation that he gave free will.

If God had declared immediately after creating mankind that man was *tôb*, then that would mean God had overridden man's free will and preprogrammed him to automatically function the way He had designed man to function. It would also mean that God changed the way He had first intended for man to mature by gaining knowledge.

Therefore, we understand that mankind exists to function in the purpose for which God designed for man and that we will not automatically function that way. We must learn what God designed us to be or do and then we must choose to be or do that. We must choose to function the way God designed us to, but this choice is a lifetime commitment. It is not enough to choose once to function in the purpose for which God created us. We must resolve that for the rest of our natural and eternal lives that we will be *tôb*.

What Is the Purpose of Mankind's Life?

So, what is God looking for from mankind?

> *But the hour is coming, and now is, when the true worshipers will worship the Father in spirit and truth; for the Father is seeking such to worship Him. John 4:23 NKJV*

The Father is seeking worshipers! He is seeking true worshipers *right now!* Could this have anything to do with the purpose for which we were made?

The only other thing I have read that God will actively search for on the earth is faith.

Nevertheless, when the Son of Man comes, will He really find faith on the earth?" Luke 18:8b NKJV

We are told here that God will be looking for faith after Jesus returns to earth. But God is looking for worshipers right now, before He returns. Worship seems to be the priority for God right now. Besides, it requires true faith to worship the Father. No one would worship a God they don't believe in.

Paul is a New Testament writer who truly understands what the purpose of mankind is. Here is how he wrote about it to the Ephesians.

> *having made known to us **the mystery of His will**, according to His good **pleasure** which He **purposed** in Himself, that in the dispensation of the fullness of the times He might gather together in one all things in Christ, both which are in heaven and which are on earth—in Him. In Him also we have obtained an inheritance, being **predestined** according to the **purpose** of Him who works all things according to the counsel of **His will**, **that we** who first trusted in Christ **should be to the praise of His glory**. Ephesians 1:9–12 KJV, emphasis added*

Here are a few important points we can derive from this passage of scripture.

- ➤ God's will for mankind is a mystery to us, which God will make known to us, if we seek Him for it.
- ➤ The purpose God has for mankind will bring Himself "good pleasure."
- ➤ God predetermined man's destiny and purpose according to His own will.
- ➤ The reason God created mankind is for us **to exist to praise the glory of God.**

This is the declared purpose of all mankind. We are to *"be to the praise of His glory."* In other words, the purpose of our life is to praise

God's glory! That is why God is seeking people to worship Him, so we will fulfill our purpose for being created.

Peter also wrote about the purpose for mankind's life in his first book.

> But ye are a chosen generation, a royal priesthood, an holy nation, a peculiar people; **that ye should show forth the praises of Him** who hath called you out of darkness into His marvelous light: 1 Peter 2:9 KJV, emphasis added

Again, the declared purpose for man's existence is to "show forth the praises of God."

The prophet Isaiah also confirmed the reason God created humanity.

> I will say to the north, `Give them up!' and to the south, `Do not hold them back.' Bring My sons from afar and My daughters from the ends of the earth – everyone who is called by My name, whom I created for My glory, whom I formed and made." Isaiah 43:6–7 NIV

Through Isaiah, God tells us that we, who are called by His Name, were created to give glory to God. This, again, is the declared reason why God created mankind. Here is one more scripture that confirms God's purpose for mankind. Please memorize this Bible verse.

> This people have I formed for Myself; **they shall show forth My praise**. Isaiah 43:21 KJV, emphasis added

The indisputable reason or purpose God created mankind was for us to worship Him or to show forth God's praise. The words "praise" and "worship" are Biblical synonyms. They basically mean the same thing. For a greater understanding of this concept, read Chapter Three of the textbook *Biblical Worship*.[7]

We are not programmed to worship God against our will—we have to make an ongoing choice to fulfill our purpose.

---

[7] Stone, S, *Biblical Worship*, 41. Bloomington: WesBow Press, 2012.

The Pronouncement of "Good" Over Mankind

Because God gave mankind a free will to choose if we will function as God designed us to function, He cannot declare that man is "good" until the end of each person's life. At that time, every person who has ever lived will stand before the "judgment seat of Christ."

> *For we must all appear before the judgment seat of Christ;*
> *that every one may receive the things done in his body,*
> *according to that he hath done, whether it be **good** or bad.*
> *2 Corinthians 5:10 KJV, emphasis added*

It is at that time that God will declare you to be "good" or not. It is at that time we will receive the judgment from Jesus Himself as to whether we functioned in the way we were designed to function.

In Matthew 25, Jesus spoke a parable about this "end-time" judgment of all of humanity.

> *"For the kingdom of heaven is like a man traveling to a*
> *far country, who called his own servants and delivered his*
> *goods to them." Matthew 25:14 (NKJV)*

This parable is talking about Jesus leaving His people on earth to do what they are supposed to do. However, Jesus will return to Earth to judge His people according to their actions.

> *After a **long** time the lord of those servants came and*
> *settled accounts with them. Matthew 25:19 NKJV,*
> *emphasis added*

Jesus will come back to Earth to see who has functioned according to their purpose and design. To some, He will report with sadness.

> *"But his lord answered and said to him, 'You wicked and*
> *lazy servant, . . . And cast the unprofitable servant into*
> *the outer darkness. There will be weeping and gnashing of*
> *teeth.' When the Son of Man comes in His glory, and all the*

holy angels with Him, then He will sit on the throne of His glory. All the nations will be gathered before Him, and He will separate them one from another, as a shepard divides his sheep from the goats. Matthew 25:26, 29–32 NKJV

What Jesus is describing here, I believe, is the judgment seat of Christ that we just discussed. At that court scene, Jesus will judge some to have functioned properly, according to their purpose.

*His lord said to him, 'Well done, **good** and faithful servant; you were faithful over a few things, I will make you ruler over many things. Enter into the joy of your lord. Matthew 25:21 NKJV, emphasis added*

Here is the *Vine's Bible Dictionary* definition for the word "good" in this scripture.

Strong's Greek Number 0018
Greek word: agathos ag-ath-os'
1) of good constitution or nature
2) useful, salutary
3) good, pleasant, agreeable, joyful, happy
4) excellent, distinguished
5) upright, honorable

As we know from our high school English class, a dictionary lists all the possible meanings of a word, but very seldom, if never, does a word mean all the definitions at the same time. We, the reader, must determine which of the meanings listed applies most in the situation. Without the prior understanding of the Hebrew word for "good," we could overlook the one *Vine's* definition that we should pay attention to—definition No. 2.

Something "salutary"[8] is "beneficial" for accomplishing a healthy or good purpose. Something is beneficial only when it functions the way it was designed to function.

---

[8] Vine's Complete Expository Dictionary.

When you stand before the judgment seat of Christ, what will you hear Him say to you? Will you have functioned on earth the way God designed you to function—as a worshiper—or will you have functioned in a selfish, self-centered way?

It is your choice as one of God's creations, made in His image, to decide within yourself to "be to the praise of His glory" or not. You must choose now on earth to be a worshiper for eternity or to substitute the true meaning of life with something very temporary. This is the only way to truly bring God pleasure as a human being, and God is searching for those who will function in the purpose for which they were designed.

My prayer for you is that you will be one of the ones to hear Jesus say to you, "Well done, **good** and faithful servant!"

God Wants Every Person to Fulfill Their Purpose

The church I grew up in taught me that Jesus' most important commandment is what we all know as the Great Commission. Here is this instruction as Matthew recorded it.

> *And when they saw him, they worshipped him: but some doubted. And Jesus came and spake unto them, saying, All power is given unto me in heaven and in earth. Go ye therefore, and teach all nations, baptizing them in the name of the Father, and of the Son, and of the Holy Ghost: Teaching them to observe all things whatsoever I have commanded you: and, lo, I am with you alway, even unto the end of the world. Amen. Matthew 28:17–20 KJV*

Because this instruction was elevated in the church I grew up in to be Jesus' most important commandment, I thought the best way to demonstrate that I was a Christian was to convince people to follow Christ. This is an important instruction from Jesus, but it is far from what Jesus calls the "greatest commandment."

As a matter of fact, Jesus never identified this final instruction as being "great" at all. Someone else called this the "Great Commission," and we have been identifying these instructions by that name for hundreds of years, based on an unidentified person's idea. The words "Great Commission" never appear in the Bible. I see Jesus' instruction more as a strategy, instead of a commandment. In it, Jesus is telling us how to tell others the "good news."

I know that the Bible teaches us that it is a smart thing to win people to the kingdom of heaven.

> *The fruit of the righteous is a tree of life; and he that winneth souls is wise. Proverbs 11:30 KJV*

But why does God want us to win people to Christ? For that matter, why does God want humans to "be fruitful and multiply," as He commanded in Genesis 1? The answer is the same for both questions.

God wants us to complete both actions so that more worshipers are on the earth. He wants every person to have the opportunity to fulfill the purpose for which he or she was created.

Chapter 2

Designed to Fulfill Our Purpose

The Importance of How God Designed Humans

Remember, every invention is designed with a specific purpose in mind. It is that design that makes the invention function for a specific purpose. The human being is no exception. How God made us has everything to do with how we accomplish our purpose for existence.

By the way, God's design for His creations is the best for accomplishing its assigned purpose. You cannot improve on God's designs! There is no elephant 2.0 or human being 2.1.

We have seen how God has created us to "show forth the praises of him who hath called you out of darkness into his marvelous light."[9] This is God's declared purpose for mankind. To understand how we are to fulfill our purpose, we must first understand how we were designed.

The Design of Humanity

"Anthropology" is the scientific term for the study of mankind. Our study in this book would fall under this scientific term.

To discover the blueprint for how God made humanity, we can consult the writings of Paul, the apostle whom the Spirit of God gave an

---

[9] 1 Pet. 2:9.

abundance of revelations.[10] In writing his prayer for the Thessalonians, Paul allows us to share in his revelation as to how God designed and created mankind.

> *And the very God of peace sanctify you **wholly**; and I pray God your whole **spirit** and **soul** and **body** be preserved blameless unto the coming of our Lord Jesus Christ. 1 Thessalonians 5:23 KJV, emphasis added*

Paul's prayer was for the whole person (*"wholly"*). Then he listed the three parts that make up a whole human being.

The Worshiper's Anthropology Chart #1

Bible Reference	The Parts of a Human Being		
1 Thessalonians 5:23	spirit	soul	body

Table VI

A Confirmation of this Design

One of the miracles of the Bible is that it confirms itself. Let's look back to the original account of creation in Genesis to see if this three-part blueprint for humanity can be verified.

> *And the LORD God formed man of the dust of the ground, and breathed into his nostrils the breath of life; and man became a living soul. Genesis 2:7 KJV*

In the creation account in Genesis, all three parts of mankind are mentioned.

Part one—The "form" of man is the body, which God created out of the dust of the earth. Remember that God had previously spoken the earth into existence; now he is forming man from that dirt.

---

[10]   2 Cor. 12:7.

Part two—The Hebrew word for "breath" in this scripture is *nashamah* [nesh-aw-maw'], which also means "spirit."[11]

Part three—Notice that the union of the dusty form of a person, and the spirit breathed into that body from almighty God, created a "living soul."

Let's match these three parts with Paul's revelation of how we are wholly made.

The Worshiper's Anthropology Chart #2

Bible Reference	The Parts of a Human Being		
1 Thessalonians 5:23	spirit	soul	body
Genesis 2:7	breath	soul	form/dust

Table VII

Notice that a human being does not exist until the spirit of life from God is joined to the physical body, causing the soul to result from the union of these two. Therefore, man is not man without all three parts of our being.

An Anthropological Controversy

There is some controversy among scholars concerning this subject. The medical profession believes that humans are two-part beings made of body and soul. They simply do not acknowledge the existence of the human spirit as a separate part of our being. To accommodate this belief in humanity, some theologians treat the words "spirit" and "soul" as interchangeable terms.

One Bible school professor I had the privilege of serving on the same faculty with taught the students that man is a two-part being, made up of body and soul. When I asked him about the human spirit, he responded that the soul and the spirit are the same thing. He based his doctrine on the translation of the Hebrew word for spirit, saying there

---

[11] Strong, J. *Strong's Exhaustive Concordance of the Bible.* (Peabody: Hendrickson Publishers, 2007).

were several times in the Old Testament where the word for spirit was translated "soul." Therefore, he concluded that these two terms were interchangeable.

When researching this theory for myself, I found the root Hebrew word for spirit is *ruwach*[12] [roo'-akh], which appears 378 times in the Old Testament and not once is it translated as "soul." The closest it comes to being translated as "soul" occurs only five times, when this word is translated into the word "mind" in the King James translation.

Even if this professor had gotten his facts straight, he violated one very important rule of hermeneutics: No translations of the scriptures are divinely inspired. The original Greek and Hebrew texts were 100 percent inspired by the Holy Spirit, which means they are infallible, not the translations of that text. I respectfully submit that it is dangerous to base any doctrine on the interpretation or translation of scripture, as my colleague did.

We have clear evidence in the scripture that God created man as a three-part being and that all three parts are equally important in the formation of a human being. Maybe my colleague was simply trying to find a way to Biblically substantiate the popular medical anthropological world view of mankind.

Another Anthropological Controversy

Another popular teaching concerning anthropology is that man *is* a spirit, who possesses a soul, and lives *in* a body. This doctrine is a widely accepted teaching, especially among Charismatic denominations and churches.

This sounds right to those who do not study the scriptures for themselves. The truth is that the form of man is just as much "man" as the spirit of man. Also, the soul is not a possession—it is just as much "man" as the spirit and the body are man. A human is only a human when it is made up of the three parts—spirit, soul, and body. If you take away any one of these three parts, we cease to be human.

---

[12] Strong, *Strong's Concordance.*

A catch phrase that this doctrine has produced goes like this: We are not physical beings having a temporary spiritual experience; we are spiritual beings having a temporary physical experience.

Although I understand the logic that would lead one to these conclusions, I respectfully submit that this is not a Biblical view of mankind. While it is true that man is a spirit being, it is also true that man *is* a "soul."

> *. . . and man became a living soul. ("being" in NIV)*
> *Genesis 2:7 KJV*

The Bible also makes it clear that our body is an integral part of our being. A thorough study of the Bible reveals that mankind cannot—and will never—exist without a body. Mankind is created in the image and likeness of God, and God is also reported to have a body.

Created in God's Likeness

God declared on the sixth day of creation that He would make mankind like Himself in two different ways.

> *Then God said, "Let Us make man in Our image, according*
> *to Our likeness. . . Genesis 1:26 NKJV*

God's image refers to God's character, which is established in a person's soul. God's likeness refers to His form, which is seen in our bodies. If you want to know what God looks like, look in the mirror. God made you in the same form and likeness He has. You have two ears and two eyes. So does God.

> *O my God, incline Your ear and hear; open Your eyes and*
> *see our desolations, and the city which is called by Your*
> *name. . . Daniel 9:18 NKJV*

You have a mouth; God has a mouth.

So then, because you are lukewarm, and neither cold nor hot, I will vomit you out of My mouth. Revelation 3:16 NKJV

You smell with your nose, and so does God.

And the Lord smelled a soothing aroma. Then the Lord said. . . Genesis 8:21 NKJV

We have eyes, ears, nose, and mouth. These parts make up the main components of a face. You have a face, and God has a face.

But your iniquities have separated between you and your God, and your sins have hid his face from you, that he will not hear. Isaiah 59:2 KJV

You have a backside, and God has a backside.

And it shall come to pass, while my glory passeth by, that I will put thee in a clift of the rock, and will cover thee with my hand while I pass by: And I will take away mine hand, and thou shalt see my back parts: but my face shall not be seen. Exodus 33:22–23 KJV

God didn't let Moses see His face, because God told Moses it would kill his body to see that much of God's glory.

And he said, Thou canst not see my face: for there shall no man see me, and live. Exodus 33:20 KJV

Instead, God let Moses see His back parts, and Moses' skin shown so bright that the people could not look at him.[13] That's how much glory God's backside has.

You have legs and feet because God has feet.

---

[13] Ex. 34:30.

"For David did not ascend into the heavens, but he says himself: The Lord said to my Lord, "Sit at My right hand, till I make Your enemies Your footstool." Acts 2:34–35 NKJV

God has a bottom that He sits on, just like you. God has a right hand; therefore, He also has a left hand, just like you. One day Jesus will prop his feet up on the devil's head, and we'll be there to see it.

By the way, Satan was not created in God's likeness like we were. In Ezekiel 28, we learn that every precious stone was Lucifer's covering,[14] not skin like God gave us. While reflecting God's glory, Lucifer would look beautiful. However, without the glory of God, Lucifer would appear as a dark, cold, hard, stony creature. This grotesque form of Lucifer was nothing without the glory of God shining on him. Yet one of Lucifer's sins was to desire to be "like" God. He was not satisfied with being who God made him to be and doing what he was created to do. Therefore, every time Satan sees a human, it reminds him that he will never be like God.

Satan hates the human race, because we look like God. Satan hates God for banishing him to the earth, yet he knows he cannot attack God directly. Therefore, he attacks God's likeness in us by attacking our bodies with all manner of sickness and infirmity.

We will discuss how mankind is made in God's image and how and why Satan attacks it in us in Chapters seven and eight. For more of an understanding as to why God created mankind like Himself and placed us on the same planet where He banished Lucifer to, read Chapter eight of *Biblical Worship*.[15]

Continuing a Previous Controversy Discussion

If we are only spirit beings, who possess a soul and live in a body, then there will be no need for a body once we leave this planet. However, the Bible makes it clear that even in heaven we will have a body like Christ's body.

---

[14] Ez. 28:12–13.
[15] Stone, S, *Biblical Worship*, 128. Bloomington: WestBow Press, 2012.

*For our conversation (way of life) is in heaven; from whence also we look for the Savior, the Lord Jesus Christ: Who shall change our **vile body**, that it may be fashioned like unto his **glorious body**, according to the working whereby he is able even to subdue all things unto himself. Philippians 3:20–21 KJV, emphasis added*

Unfortunately, not everyone will be going to heaven. Even if hell is our destination, we will still have a body there as well.

*And if thy right **eye** offend thee, pluck it out, and cast it from thee: for it is profitable for thee that one of thy members should perish, and not that thy whole **body** should be cast into hell. Matthew 5:29 KJV, emphasis added*

*And in hell he lift up his **eyes**, being in torments, and seeth Abraham afar off, and Lazarus in his **bosom**. Luke 16:23 KJV, emphasis added*

Human life cannot exist anywhere without a spirit and a body, because the union of these becomes a living soul. The great Chinese Christian martyr and theologian, Watchman Nee, declared that our soul is the "seat" of our personality.[16] Scientific technology has finally developed to the place where we can actually observe with sonograms the physical body of a baby—and even the personality—developing in the womb. This then is evidence that the child's spirit is present, since the soul cannot exist without the union of the spirit and body.

Yet Another Anthropological Controversy

Just as our bodies have their origin at conception, so does our spirit. To believe we existed in heaven as a spirit being before our conception on Earth is to believe one of the fundamental teachings of reincarnation. This doctrine is at the root of many of the occult based religions, as well as the false "Christian" cults, such as Mormonism.

---

[16] Nee, W, *The Spiritual Man*, Vol. 1. New York: Christian Fellowship, Inc., 1977.

God breathed spirit into Adam and Eve at the time He formed their bodies, not before. That is God's pattern for creating human life. He breaths spiritual life into every human, at the moment the body is conceived. The union of spirit and flesh becomes a living soul or a human "being."

With all due respect to the Christians who have been deceived into believing that their spirit existed before conception and that we will exist in the future without a body, I submit that these teachings have their roots in "doctrines of demons,"[17] not the Word of God. For further understanding of this concept, please read 1 Corinthians 15:35–44.

Three Parts of God, Three Parts of Man

The conclusion of this study is that mankind is, and will always be, a three-part being, since God is a three-part being and we are made in His image. God is Spirit, Father, and Word. God cannot exist without each part or he would cease to be God. Likewise, without all three parts of man, humanity ceases to be human.

> *For there are three that bear record in heaven, the Father,*
> *the Word, and the Holy Ghost: and these three are one.*
> *And there are three that bear witness in earth, the Spirit,*
> *and the water, and the blood: and these three agree in one.*
> *1 John 5:7–8 KJV*

The Human Body

The body of a human being lives in water the first nine months of life. Our bodies are made up of about 80 percent water. For these reasons, we equate the body with the water in this scripture.

The Human Soul

Since life is thought of as more than physical by the Eastern mind and since it was thought that blood was the fluid of life, including both

---

[17] 1 Tim. 4:1.

the physical life and the "soulish" life as well, we equate the blood with the soul.

The Human Spirit

Obviously, it takes no further understanding to equate the spirit with the Holy Spirit in this scripture.

Our Biblical Anthropological Chart continues to grow as verification of the blueprint or design God used for creating mankind.

The Worshiper's Anthropology Chart #3

Bible Reference	The Parts of a Human Being		
1 Thessalonians 5:23	spirit	soul	body
Genesis 2:7	breath	soul	form/dust
1 John 5:7 (God)	Holy Ghost	Father	Word
1 John 5:8 (man)	spirit	blood	water

Table VIII

Once again, we have verified that without all three parts of our being we would cease to be made in God's image and likeness. All three parts make up a person. Without any one of these parts, we cease to be a human made in God's image.

One more quick thought about this scripture: Just as Jesus, The Word, is the "express image" of God,[18] so is our body the expresser of both our soul and our spirit.

The Human Soul

Although there is not a specific definition of the soul found neatly packaged within scripture, it is not difficult to understand the soul through a thorough searching of the scriptures and by revelation from the Spirit of God. Many wonderful men and women of God have put forth their revelations concerning the human soul, yet most theologians

---

[18] Heb. 1:3

of the twentieth century and beyond have recognized the definition offered by Watchman Nee in the first book of a three-volume set entitled *The Spiritual Man* as a non-improvable definition of the human soul.

Watchman Nee says the soul is ". . . the seat of his/man's personality. . . . That which constitutes a man's personality are the main faculties of volition, mind, and emotions."[19] This chart shows the trichotomy of the human soul, as defined by Watchman Nee.

The Worshiper's Anthropology Chart #4 The Soul

1 Thessalonians 5:23	spirit	soul	body
	Will	Mind	Emotions

Table IX

Although many have tried, no one has been able to come up with a better and more-succinct definition of the human soul than this. Therefore, we will use this definition of the soul throughout the rest of this book.

Instinctively We Worship

You may recall from Chapter one that mankind was the only part of creation that God had to instruct about eating. Most of what we humans do to sustain and protect life must be learned from our parents. Mankind was made to grow, or progress, according to the knowledge we gain throughout our lives. God has given the rest of creation preprogrammed instincts to help them function. Mankind might be able to train creatures to do certain actions, but without a sense of reason that God gave to man, that's as far as it can go.

There is one thing that God did preprogram mankind to do, however. God has given man the instinct to worship. Because of this, humans will always worship something or someone, without exception.

---

[19] Nee, *Spiritual Man.*

Just as God programmed the geese to fly south for the winter, the bears to hibernate, the trees to release their leaves in season, and the salmon to swim upstream, God has programmed human beings to worship. It is impossible for a human being to not worship something or someone. Even individuals who do not recognize the existence of God will instinctively find something they can direct worship to. This could be a nonreligious idol, such as possessions, a position, another person, or prosperity itself. It could also be ideals and Philosophies, knowledge, expertise, an experience (realized or unrealized), a human or fantasy relationship, and on, and on the list could go.

According to Dr. Lawrence J. Crabb Jr., noted Christian psychologist, God has programmed mankind with two basic needs. Here is an excerpt from *The Training Manual for the Institute of Biblical Counseling* written by him.

> *"Biblical Counselors must be aware that they are dealing with persons whose personal needs are not being met, and who therefore are showing troublesome evidence of personal breakdown. What are the personal needs which relentlessly demand satisfaction:*
>
> *1. "Security*
> *"A convinced awareness of being unconditionally and totally loved without needing to change in order to win love, loved by a love which is freely given, which cannot be earned and therefore cannot be lost.*
>
> *2. "Significance*
> *"A realization of personal adequacy for a job which is truly important, a job which fundamentally involves having a meaningful impact on another person.*
>
> *"The core of the entire approach to counseling assumed in the IBC Manual is this: OUR PERSONAL NEEDS FOR SECURITY AND SIGNIFICANCE CAN ONLY BE GENUINELY AND FULLY MET IN RELATIONSHIP WITH JESUS CHRIST."[20]*

[20] Crabb, Lawrence J., Jr, *Institute of Biblical Counseling: Training Manual*, 11. Colorado, 1978.

In the training sessions, Crabb identified these two needs in this scripture.

> *So God created man in his own image, in the image of God created he him; male and female created he them. And God blessed them, and God said unto them, be fruitful, and multiply, and replenish the earth, and subdue it: and have dominion over the fish of the sea, and over the fowl of the air, and over every living thing that moveth upon the earth. Genesis 1:27–28 KJV*

The first instinctive need God programmed into humanity, according to Crabb, was met by God when "God blessed them." This instinct is the need for **security**. Every human needs a sense of security, which can only be fulfilled through a relationship with Jesus. Still, millions of people try to find their security in the things they have filled their lives with.

> *Some trust in chariots, and some in horses: but we will remember the name of the LORD our God. They are brought down and fallen: but we are risen, and stand upright. Psalms 20:7–8 KJV*

I'm sure you have seen those who have worked for a company all their lives, placing their security in their pension, only to lose everything when the company went out of business. Some place their hope in the stock market or other investments, only to lose everything in one day. Nothing in this world is secure. The only security in this life is the blessing of the Almighty God.

God programmed the need for security within every human to compel us to seek a relationship with Him. The expression of our love to God through worship should flow freely, since He provides the security for our lives.

The second instinctive need that God programmed within humanity, according to Crabb, is a need for **significance**. The privilege of being created in the image of God carries with it a certain level of responsibility according to this scripture.

. . . and God said unto them, be fruitful, and multiply, and replenish the earth, and subdue it: and have dominion over the fish of the sea, and over the fowl of the air, and over every living thing that moveth upon the earth. Genesis 1:28 KJV

Here God specifically instructed Adam and Eve about their responsibilities, saying they were first of all to have children. Also, in areas where the natural course of events has resulted in an area of depletion, man is to "replenish" the earth. Finally, mankind was to subdue the earth and have dominion over every part of it.

Since we know that all of creation exists *only* to glorify God and, therefore, bring Him pleasure, we then realize how mankind's significance is to be wrapped up in seeing God receive maximum glory from us and all His creation.

It is not a little thing to bring pleasure to the Creator of all that exists in the universe. When you think that your praise can move His heart, you begin to realize how significant you are to Him and that there can be no greater significance in life than to worship your creator/God!

Because of these two fundamental needs that God has programmed into every human, we are compelled by them to experience their fulfillment. Yet, there is no greater significance in life than to move God's heart through the expression of our love for God. Likewise, there is no greater security in life than the blessing of Almighty God, which comes to us when we truly worship Him with all of our being.

Therefore, because of these two preprogrammed, instinctive human needs, mankind will always give our passion and love to something or someone without fail! Likewise, these needs also drive mankind to seek out an object for our worship.

The Sacrifice of Praise

Throughout scripture, worship of God is always associated with sacrifice. In the Old Testament, these sacrifices were the blood of innocent animals. In the New Testament, the blood of Jesus was the last blood sacrifice needed to pay for our relationship with God. However, worship is still associated with sacrifice for New Testament Christians. That which dies now in our worship of God is our flesh.

> *By him therefore let us offer the **sacrifice of praise** to God continually, that is, the fruit of our **lips** giving thanks to his name. Hebrews 13:15 KJV, emphasis added*

Our praise to God is a sacrifice for us, because our flesh wars against the Spirit of God, who is in us. The first member of our being that is required to act in a sacrificial way is our lips—or as James calls it, our tongue.[21] These are the parts of our body associated with speech. In other words, the first level of the sacrifice of praise for our flesh begins with our mouth, expressing thankfulness to Jesus for being our Lord and Savior.

> *That if thou shalt confess with thy **mouth** the Lord Jesus, and shalt believe in thine heart that God hath raised him from the dead, thou shalt be saved. For with the heart man believeth unto righteousness; and with the **mouth** confession is made unto salvation. Romans 10:9–10 KJV, emphasis added*

Everyone's sacrifice of praise starts with the mouth. However, as we grow in the Lord, we are required to progress to where our sacrifice of praise is expressed with our entire body.

> *Therefore, I urge you, brothers, in view of God's mercy, to offer your **bodies** as living **sacrifices**, holy and pleasing to God—this is your spiritual act of worship. Romans 12:1 NIV, emphasis added*

It can be a real sacrifice for our flesh to express love to God with our body. Yet, this is what God eventually expects from us all. Therefore, our sacrifice of praise is progressive. It starts with our mouth at salvation

---

[21] James 3:1–12.

and then progresses to other parts of our body being used to express our love to God.

Physical expressions of worship are expressed through both postures and actions. Examples of expressing worship with postures are kneeling or laying prostrate before God. Examples of worship actions are clapping or dancing before God. All these are Biblical expressions of love to God, yet not all of us are comfortable expressing ourselves in these ways. This is why it is called the sacrifice of praise.

Again, remember, if we do not sacrifice ourselves for God, we will give our passion sacrificially to something or someone else. God has programmed us to need to worship. Whatever we direct our affection to, if it is not the Lord God, it will eventually destroy us.

> He that sacrificeth unto any god, save unto the LORD
> only, he shall be utterly destroyed. Exodus 22:20 KJV

Let me say this again, choosing to not worship God through Jesus Christ will result in complete destruction and alienation from God for eternity.

Worship Is the Expression of Love to God

In Chapter Two of *Biblical Worship*, we established that Christianity and Judaism are the only two religions in the world where the relationship between God and mankind is based on love. All other world religions are fear-based, where man must appease his god for fear of retaliation. In reality, Judaism also becomes fear-based, because of the Law. Jesus came and changed all of that with His grace and mercy, by paying the price for our sins. Because of Jesus, it is possible for us to know and experience God's true love.

> And we have known and believed the love that God hath
> to us. God is love; and he that dwelleth in love dwelleth in
> God, and God in him. Herein is our love made perfect, that
> we may have boldness in the day of judgment: because as
> he is, so are we in this world. There is no fear in love; but

perfect love casteth out fear: because fear hath torment. He that feareth is not made perfect in love. We love him, because he first loved us. 1 John 4:16–19 KJV

The angels in heaven worship God. Why was that not enough for the Lord? It is because they were not made in God's image. They were not made with the ability to love. They were never intended to become the children of God or to have a love relationship with God. Only humans were created for these things.

Commanded to Worship

Because mankind only grows by increasing in knowledge, the Lord gave us specific instructions on how to function. He calls them "commandments." The commandments God gives are never for His benefit—they are to guide us to discover important behavior that will sustain and advance our lives as human beings. In the following story, Jesus guides a lawyer to discover a very important commandment.

> *And, behold, a certain lawyer stood up, and tempted him, saying, Master, what shall I do to inherit eternal life?*
>
> *He said unto him, What is written in the law? how readest thou?*
>
> *And he answering said, Thou shalt love the Lord thy God with all thy heart, and with all thy soul, and with all thy strength, and with all thy mind; and thy neighbor as thyself.*
>
> *And he (Jesus) said unto him, Thou hast answered right: this do, and thou shalt live. Luke 10:25–28 KJV*

Notice Jesus' words and how strong they are. He is saying that, if we express our love to God in worship, *we will live*, implying that if we do not love God, we will die.

Since Jesus is "life,"[22] our only source of life as human beings is to be connected to Him in a love relationship and to express that love to Him

---

[22] John 14:6.

through worship with our entire being. This is what He has commanded us to do in His greatest commandment, because He knows that if we do not do this, we will die.

The Law of First Mention

Hermeneutics means "the science of interpretation, especially of the Scriptures."[23] One very dynamic hermeneutic technique we all should be aware of is called "The Law of First Mention." Quite simply, this technique says that if you go to the first place in scripture where something is mentioned, you will always discover something very important concerning the topic you are studying that will not always be evident in the other references to that topic throughout the Bible.

To demonstrate this, let's find the first place in scripture where the word "prophet" is used. The correlation of this short side study to the study of worship will become evident at a later time; but for now, let's simply find out who the first prophet in the Bible was.

The story goes like this. Abraham and Sarah were traveling to a new place, which they were not yet certain where it was. They were going simply out of obedience to the Lord, who told them to go. In their travels, they passed through a kingdom ruled by King Abimelech. Now Sarah, the Bible tells us, was a good-looking lady, and word on the streets was that the king was looking for a new wife, because none of his other wives were able to bear him an heir. Abraham, afraid that King Abimelech would kill him and take Sarah for his next wife, talked Sarah into agreeing to tell everybody that they were brother and sister and not husband and wife. I guess he figured this barbaric king would take Sarah either way, but this way he would get to live.

Well, as suspected, King Abimelech informed them that Sarah would be his new wife, and he took her away from Abraham to live in his dwelling. However, before the wedding took place, God visited Abimelech at night. His greeting was blunt and to the point.

---

[23] hermeneutics. Dictionary.com. *Dictionary.com Unabridged*. Random House, Inc. http://www.dictionary.com/browse/hermeneutics (accessed: October 10, 2017).

But God came to Abimelech in a dream by night, and said to him, Behold, thou art but a dead man, for the woman which thou hast taken; for she is a man's wife. Genesis 20:3 KJV

Abimelech quickly realized that his decisions were under the Almighty God's scrutiny, and now we see a king—who feared no one and who's reputation was that he would not hesitate to kill to have what he wanted—face to face with the God of the universe, fearing for his own life. Abimelech would have done anything God told him to do at that point, just to save his life. Here are God's instructions to him.

*Now therefore restore the man his wife; for he is a **prophet**, and he shall **pray** for thee, and thou shalt live: and if thou restore her not, know thou that thou shalt surely die, thou, and all that are thine. Genesis 20:7 KJV, emphasis added*

This is the first time the word "prophet" is used in scripture. God is the first to use this word and does so to reference His covenant friend Abraham. In addition to this discovery, it is very interesting to find out that this is the very first time in the Bible the word "pray" was used in reference to asking God for something. From the first mention of "prophet" and "pray" in scripture, we conclude that the first assigned responsibility for a God-appointed prophet was intercession [*he shall pray for thee*]. Because of this, I believe the first responsibility of any person who is prophetic is to pray for the people whom God has revealed things about to you.

It seems to me that, these days, we have a lot of self-proclaimed prophets in Christendom who like to spout the "Word of the Lord" yet find it beneath them to intercede for others. I believe, based on the authority of this scripture, that a true prophet of God is first and foremost an intercessor for others. I believe it is less important to run and tell someone what God has revealed to us about that individual than it is for us to take that "word of knowledge" or "prophesy" and begin to pray for that person in our prayer closet.

The Greatest Commandment and First Mention

We just read the account in Luke where Jesus identified for us the greatest commandment. Here is that same story from Matthew's perspective.

> *Then one of them, which was a lawyer, asked him a question, tempting him, and saying, Master, which is the great commandment in the law?*
> *Jesus said unto him, Thou shalt love the Lord thy God with all thy heart, and with all thy soul, and with all thy mind. This is the first and great commandment. And the second is like unto it, Thou shalt love thy neighbor as thyself. On these two commandments hang all the law and the prophets. Matt 22:35–40 KJV*

After reading this story in these two different gospels, I noticed that they both had a slightly different list of components to love God with. Luke's list is heart, soul, strength, and mind, while Matthew's list is heart, soul, and mind. This prompted me to look up this commandment in other places in the Bible.

I found that in Deuteronomy 10:12, 11:13, 13:3, 30:6 and in Joshua 22:5, the only two components mentioned are heart and soul. This is not meant to be an exhaustive list of scriptures where the greatest commandment occurs, I am simply making the point that throughout scripture the lists of the parts of our being vary wherever this commandment is mentioned.

To my former colleague who believed that the words "spirit/heart" and "soul" are interchangeable, why would God differentiate between these two parts so many times if they were the same thing?

For the sake of discovery, let's look at the first place in the Bible where this commandment appears, applying the hermeneutic law of first mention to see what we can discover.

> *Now these are the commandments, the statutes, and the judgments, which the LORD your God commanded to*

teach you, that ye might do them in the land whither ye go to possess it: That thou mightest fear the LORD thy God, to keep all his statutes and his commandments, which I command thee, thou, and thy son, and thy son's son, all the days of thy life; and that thy days may be prolonged.

*Hear therefore, O Israel, and observe to do it; that it may be well with thee, and that ye may increase mightily, as the LORD God of thy fathers hath promised thee, in the land that floweth with milk and honey. Hear, O Israel: The LORD our God is one LORD: And thou shalt love the LORD thy God with all thine **heart**, and with all thy **soul**, and with all thy **might**. And these words, which I command thee this day, shall be in thine heart: Deuteronomy 6:1–6 KJV, emphasis added*

The first time the great commandment is given in scripture, we see that God is commanding us to love Him with the same three parts of our being that He created us with.

The word "heart" is literally translated "the middle" or "center" of our being. Since we understand that it is central to the creation of a human being to have God breath spirit-life into us at conception, we equate these two words—"heart" and "spirit"—as the same thing.

Watchman Nee has already defined the word "soul" for us, so it needs no further explanation.

The word "might," or "strength" as Jesus referred to it in the Gospel of Luke, refers to the human body. The Greeks used to worship the human body's strength. As a matter of fact, our current summer Olympics, which take place every four years, are based on the ancient Greek worship of the strength capable by the human body.

So, what we learn using the law of first mention in this case is that the greatest commandment God has ever given us is to express love to Him with all three parts of our being, which He created us with. This is very important to understand! God has always had a way He wants to be worshiped. Now we are learning that the way God created us has everything to do with how He wants us to worship Him. It takes all three parts of our being to worship God His way.

We cannot simply say we will worship God in our spirit or in our mind only. *Partial worship is not Biblical worship!* God created us in three parts to show forth His praise. Therefore, we conclude that He wants all three parts of our being involved when we worship Him. But in case we didn't get that, He made His greatest commandment to us crystal clear—that He wants us to love Him with every part of our being.

The Worshiper's Anthropology Chart #5

Bible Reference	The Parts of a Human Being		
1 Thessalonians 5:23	spirit	soul	body
Genesis 2:7	breath	soul	form/dust
1 John 5:8	spirit	blood	water
Deuteronomy 6:5	heart	soul	might

Table X

Chapter 3

Salvation to Fulfill Our Purpose

Death Through Disobedience

So far in this book, we have come to understand that mankind was created by God for the purpose of praising God.

> This people have I formed for Myself; they shall show forth My praise. Isaiah 43:21 KJV

Next, we discovered that the reason God made us in three parts is so that we can fulfill the purpose for which He made us. That means all three parts of a human being are necessary for praising Him. Because it is so important that we express our love for God using our spirit, soul, and body, God made this his greatest commandment.

> And thou shalt love the LORD thy God with all thine heart, and with all thy soul, and with all thy might. Deuteronomy 6:5 KJV

The way God designed and made us has everything to do with how we fulfill our purpose.

However, right after mankind was created, the "tempter" challenged God's instructions to man, resulting in death to mankind.

> *Then the Lord God took the man and put him in the garden of Eden to tend and keep it. And the Lord God commanded the man, saying, "Of every tree of the garden you may freely eat; but of the tree of the knowledge of good and evil you shall not eat, for in the day that you eat of it you shall surely die." Genesis 2:15–17 NKJV*

> *Then the serpent said to the woman, "You will not surely die." Genesis 3:4 NKJV*

Here's a question for you: Which of the three parts of man died when Adam and Eve sinned by eating from the forbidden tree? Was it the spirit, the soul, or the body? The answer is actually that all three parts died. The spirit died immediately. Then, without the influence of God's Spirit in their lives, their soul died progressively by the curse of the death of this world. Finally, their bodies began to slowly decay, just like our bodies do now from the day we are born. Eventually our bodies wear out and die, just like theirs did.

Here's the next question: Which part of our being did God redeem by sending Jesus to die on the cross? The answer is that Jesus purchased all three parts of our beings with His blood.

> *Or do you not know that your body is the temple of the Holy Spirit who is in you, whom you have from God, and you are not your own? For you were bought at a price; therefore glorify God in your body and in your spirit, which are God's. 1 Corinthians 6:19–20 NKJV*

Notice the reason Jesus redeemed us was so we could "glorify God." That means Jesus redeemed us so we could fulfill our original purpose for being created. Although this scripture only mentions the body and the spirit, we need to remember it is the union of the body and Spirit that makes a human soul.

The Redemption Plan

Because Adam sinned, all of mankind has been born into sin, with a sin nature, separated from a love relationship with the Almighty God. Because of this, God initiated a redemption plan by which He could be brought back into a love relationship with mankind. This redemption plan involved God taking on the form of His creation and paying the price necessary to redeem us back from the bondage of sin that had enslaved us.

It only took one man (Adam) to alienate all of mankind from God, and it only took one manifestation of God to fix the problem. Therefore, there is only one way to be reconciled with God.

> *For since by man came death, by man came also the resurrection of the dead. For as in Adam all die, even so in Christ shall all be made alive. 1 Corinthians 15:21–22 KJV*

> *And all things are of God, who hath reconciled us to himself by Jesus Christ, and hath given to us the ministry of reconciliation; To wit, that God was in Christ, reconciling the world unto himself, not imputing their trespasses unto them; and hath committed unto us the word of reconciliation. 2 Corinthians 5:18–19 KJV*

These scriptures are in the King James translation of the Bible. The English language has definitely changed a lot since then. For instance, I have not heard anyone use the phrase "to wit" in conversation lately. This old English phrase simply means "which means."

Redeemed to Fulfill the Purpose

Mankind was created for the purpose of showing forth the glory of God. Mankind chose, by his free will, to disobey God—thereby cutting himself off from God.

Even though mankind had rejected God, God chose to pursue us and set a plan in motion to redeem us back to Himself, so we would have another chance to fulfill the purpose for which He created us.

Here is Paul's explanation of God's redemption plan, which Paul wrote to the Ephesians.

Blessed be the God and Father of our Lord Jesus Christ, who hath blessed us with all spiritual blessings in heavenly places in Christ:

According as he hath chosen us in him before the foundation of the world, that we should be holy and without blame before him in love:

Having predestinated us unto the adoption of children by Jesus Christ to himself, according to the good pleasure of his will,

To the praise of the glory of his grace, wherein he hath made us accepted in the beloved.

In whom we have redemption through his blood, the forgiveness of sins, according to the riches of his grace;

Wherein he hath abounded toward us in all wisdom and prudence;

Having made known unto us the mystery of his will, according to his good pleasure which he hath purposed in himself:

That in the dispensation of the fullness of times he might gather together in one all things in Christ, both which are in heaven, and which are on earth; even in him:

In whom also we have obtained an inheritance, being predestinated according to the purpose of him who worketh all things after the counsel of his own will:

That we should be to the praise of his glory, who first trusted in Christ.

In whom ye also trusted, after that ye heard the word of truth, the gospel of your salvation: in whom also after that ye believed, ye were sealed with that holy Spirit of promise,

> *Which is the earnest of our inheritance until the*
> *redemption of the purchased possession, unto the praise*
> *of his glory. Ephesians 1:3–14 KJV*

God's purchased possession is you—your spirit, soul, and body. The reason God purchased you was "unto the praise of his glory." Again, this is the same reason he made you in the first place.

God's will is that mankind should be to "the praise of his glory." We were created to praise His glory, and we were redeemed to praise His glory. That is our purpose for being.

God's Spirit joined to our spirit is just the down payment of our inheritance from God, which is the redemption of the rest of our being as well.

Anyone who buys and sells real estate is familiar with the word "earnest," which simply means a down payment to show how serious the buyer is about making the purchase. God is very earnest about redeeming our entire being to Himself. To show us how serious He is, at the moment we ask Him to be Lord of our lives, He gives us His Holy Spirit, which He joins to our spirit so we will know that one day He will take delivery on the rest of our being as well, which is the full "purchased possession." When that happens, the redemption plan will be completed, and forever we will be "unto the praise of his glory" for all of eternity.

Deliverance from the Power of Darkness

Part of our inheritance as God's children is deliverance from the power of darkness on all three levels of our being—spirit, soul, and body. This is the reason for God's redemption plan, which God implemented through Jesus.

> *Giving thanks unto the Father, which hath made us meet*
> *(fitting) to be partakers of the inheritance of the saints in*
> *light: Who hath delivered us from the power of darkness,*
> *and hath translated us into the kingdom of his dear Son:*
> *In whom we have redemption through his blood, even the*
> *forgiveness of sins: Colossians 1:12–14 KJV*

My first thought from this scripture is that it is God who qualifies us to receive our inheritance as His children.

Second, his redemption plan can be summed up this way: God took on human form so He could demonstrate His love for mankind through the miracles He did and the suffering He bore. Through this, He paid the price to redeem mankind from being the slave of sin. This price was the shedding of His own blood. Since the price was paid to satisfy justice against sin, if we accept Jesus as our supreme sacrifice for our sins, our sins are forgiven.

Let me demonstrate with scriptures exactly how the Lord has planned to redeem all three parts of our being. Let's begin with our spirit.

A Christian's Spirit Has Been Delivered

When we invite Jesus to be Lord of our lives, He joins His Holy Spirit to our human spirit. This gives life to our dead spirit, and the two spirits become one Spirit.

> But he that is joined unto the Lord is one spirit. 1 Corinthians 6:17 KJV

Once this has occurred, Paul refers to this union in the Bible as "the Spirit," as contrasted with "the flesh."

> For what the law could not do in that it was weak through the flesh, God did by sending His own Son in the likeness of sinful flesh, on account of sin: He condemned sin in the flesh, that the righteous requirement of the law might be fulfilled in us who do not walk according to the flesh but according to **the Spirit**. For those who live according to the flesh set their minds on the things of the flesh, but those who live according to **the Spirit**, the things of **the Spirit**. Romans 8:3–5 NKJV, emphasis added

Where the Spirit of God is there is wholeness. Where the Spirit of God is there is completeness. Where the Spirit of God is there is liberty, healing, provision, sanctification, the fruit of the Spirit, the gifts of the Spirit, comfort, miracles, and love. There is no lack where the Spirit of God is! With our spirit joined to God's Spirit, our spirit is completely saved or delivered. It will never be more saved than it is right now!

Let's read this scripture one more time, remembering that Jesus dwells in us, or in our being, by joining His Spirit with our spirit. Since our spirit is part of us, and is inside our body, then God's Spirit comes to live there as well.

> *What? know ye not that your body is the temple of the Holy Ghost which is in you, which ye have of God, and ye are not your own? For ye are bought with a price: therefore glorify God in your body, and in your spirit, which are God's. 1 Corinthians 6:19–20 KJV*

The Holy Spirit lives in us, inside our body, when we have made Jesus Lord of our lives. Christ's Spirit is inside our body because He dwells in our "hearts," and our heart (or spirit) is contained within our body.

> *That he would grant you, according to the riches of his glory, to be strengthened with might by his Spirit in the inner man; That Christ may dwell in your hearts by faith; that ye, being rooted and grounded in love, Ephesians 3:16–17 KJV*

In this scripture, we learn that God's Spirit, ministering strength to our "inner man," is the same thing as Christ dwelling in our hearts. In other words, Christ is the Holy Spirit dwelling in our spirit. This is also confirmed by Jesus' very words as He explained to His disciples what will happen when He leaves them.

> *And I will pray the Father, and he shall give you another Comforter, that he may abide with you forever; even the Spirit of truth; whom the world cannot receive, because it seeth him not, neither knoweth him: but ye know him; for he dwelleth with you, and shall be in you. I will not leave*

*you comfortless: **I** will come to you. John 14:16–18 KJV, emphasis added*

Christ dwelling in our spirit is the same thing as the Spirit of God, or the Spirit of Truth, abiding in our body. Some theologians believe that there are two major experiences in Christians' lives: the day we receive Christ as our Lord and Savior and the day we receive the Holy Spirit. This second experience is sometimes called the "baptism of the Holy Spirit" or being "filled" with the Spirit. Great pain is taken by some to theologically establish a second experience wherein we receive the Holy Spirit subsequent to receiving Christ. Such teaching is not at all Biblical. In fact, Paul makes this point very clear in the book of Romans.

*But ye are not in the flesh, but in the Spirit, if so be that the Spirit of God dwell in you. Now if any man have not the Spirit of **Christ**, he is none of his. Romans 8:9 KJV, emphasis added*

According to this scripture, if the "Spirit of Christ," which is the "Spirit of God," is not in us, we are not a child of God, we are not one of His. Since we are only considered a Christian when we have the Holy Spirit joined to our spirit, it makes it impossible for us to receive the Holy Spirit after salvation. Again, I say, our spirit becomes one with God's Spirit the moment we make Jesus Lord of our lives, and our spirit will never be more saved, sanctified, or delivered than it is at that moment.

There is, however, a second experience subsequent to salvation that involves the Holy Spirit. According to Jesus, this is not an experience where we receive the Holy Spirit but one where the Spirit is released from within us.

In the last day, that great day of the feast, Jesus stood and cried, saying, If any man thirst, let him come unto me, and drink. He that believeth on me, as the scripture hath said, out of his belly shall flow rivers of living water. (But this spake he of the Spirit, which they that believe on him should receive: for the Holy Ghost was not yet

*given; because that Jesus was not yet glorified.) John
7:37–39 KJV*

The word "belly" is also translated "inner most being" in some translations of the Bible. According to Ephesians 3:16, our "inner man" is our spirit. Therefore, it is safe to state that out of our "Spirit" will flow these spiritual rivers of living water, which is the Holy Spirit.

The "baptism of the Holy Spirit" occurs when the Spirit gushes out from inside us with force, like a river, with such great volume that we are enveloped or swallowed up in His presence. The original meaning of the word "baptized" carried with it the idea of being totally submerged in water. That's what God wants to do with us with His Spirit. He wants to saturate us inside the presence of His Holy Spirit, which has been released from inside us.

Some theologians believe that the day of Pentecost was the day Jesus' disciples received the Holy Spirit for the first time; as such, theologians feel that there is only one experience we are to seek. These people believe that the Pentecostal experience was both their day of salvation and the day they were "baptized with the Holy Spirit," making these two experiences one in the same. This is the account of that first Pentecostal experience.

> *And when the day of Pentecost was fully come, they were
> all with one accord in one place. And suddenly there came
> a sound from heaven as of a rushing mighty wind, and
> it filled all the house where they were sitting. And there
> appeared unto them cloven tongues like as of fire, and it
> sat upon each of them. And they were all filled with the
> Holy Ghost, and began to speak with other tongues, as the
> Spirit gave them utterance. Acts 2:1–4 KJV*

But the Day of Pentecost was not when the disciples received the Spirit of Christ. Pentecost was the day when the Spirit was released out of their bellies. So, when was it that Jesus gave the disciples the Spirit?

> *Then the same day at evening, being the first day of the week, when the doors were shut where the disciples were assembled for fear of the Jews, came Jesus and stood in the midst, and saith unto them, Peace be unto you. And when he had so said, he shewed unto them his hands and his side. Then were the disciples glad, when they saw the Lord. Then said Jesus to them again, Peace be unto you: as my Father hath sent me, even so send I you. And when he had said this, **he breathed on them**, and saith unto them, **Receive ye the Holy Ghost**: John 20:19–22 KJV, emphasis added*

Salvation or deliverance for our spirit occurs at the moment we confess Jesus is our Lord. That is when Jesus gives us His Spirit, which joins to our spirit. After that salvation experience, we are filled with the Spirit when the Spirit is released from inside us to "well up" until we are saturated with, and enveloped by, the Holy Spirit.

This subsequent experience to salvation of being "filled" with the Holy Spirit should occur many times in our lives.

> *And be not drunk with wine, wherein is excess; but be filled with the Spirit; Ephesians 5:18 KJV*

The word "filled" in Greek is in present tense. This means that this commandment is for the present moment only. In other words, it doesn't matter how much we have been filled with the Spirit in the past, that does not qualify as obedience to this commandment. The only thing that matters is how full we are of the Holy Spirit at any given moment.

Regardless of whether you have experienced being filled or baptized with the Holy Spirit by the release of the Holy Spirit from within you, this experience has nothing to do with salvation. With our spirit joined to God's, our spirit is completely saved or delivered. Again, it will never be more saved than it is right now!

The Soul Is in the Process of Being Delivered

It is clear from the scriptures, and the revelations of men like Watchman Nee, that our mind comprises the major part of our soul. Therefore, it is safe to say that whatever affects our mind effects our soul and whatever affects our soul affects our mind. In fact, I believe it is quite legitimate to interchange these two words (mind and soul).

The reason for me saying this is because the emotions and the will can both be considered as functions of the mind. To make a choice, or exercise your will, requires a decision—which is a function of the mind. That's why we say "My mind is made up" when we exercise our will. Also, emotions are a part of every memory file in our mind. Not only do we remember the facts about everything we live through, but we also remember how we felt about that situation. Therefore, we conclude that our mind is our soul.

Concerning salvation, our mind must undergo a process of deliverance while we are on this earth. Our soul is not automatically delivered or saved at the time our spirit is. This is a very important concept for us to grasp. If we do not understand this point, it will cause us much grief as we attempt to grow in the Lord.

> *And be not conformed to this world: but be ye transformed by the renewing of your mind, that ye may prove what is that good, and acceptable, and perfect, will of God.*
> *Romans 12:2 KJV*

Without the influence of God's Spirit being one with our spirit, our soul has no choice but to conform to the world's way of thinking and doing things. The world's way is the way of our flesh or the way of our natural man. However, once our spirit is saved, then we no longer have to be a slave to our flesh or to the world's pattern. Because the spirit of God is now resident within our being, we now have the power to overcome the strength of our flesh. Now we can begin to change our way of thinking to the way Christ thinks.

That ye put off concerning the former conversation the old man, which is corrupt according to the deceitful lusts; And be renewed in the spirit ("attitude" in NIV) of your mind; Ephesians 4:22–23 KJV

To have our soul renewed requires a process that the scripture calls being "transformed." Transformation implies a process of change from one state of being to another over a period of time. The time allowed for us to experience this transformation is the time we live here on earth.

The way we are transformed (changed through a process) is to have our mind (our soul) renewed. Perhaps it would make more sense to the twenty-first century mind to use the word "reprogrammed" instead of "renewed." Our mind is a highly sophisticated computer. All computers must be programmed to work properly. Our minds have been programmed according to the world's ways (the way of the flesh) since the day we were conceived. Now that we have given our lives over to the Lordship of Jesus Christ, our minds now must be reprogrammed by God's Spirit according to the Word of God.

For example, I was in Vietnam when I committed my life to Jesus Christ. As detailed in the preface, a young man—Don Elliot—led me to the Lord and discipled me in Christ for the year I was in that country.

Note: A discipler is simply one who makes sure you are reprogramming your mind according to God's Spiritual influence. A disciple is one who has committed himself or herself to be accountable to someone who will make sure he or she is reprogramming the mind.

I loved Don! He had taught me so much and helped me to grow in Christ as a baby Christian. However, Don could see that my trust was transferring from Jesus to him, and that troubled him, so he sought God for wisdom as to how to teach me a lesson and bring my focus back onto Jesus. One day we were at a picnic on the beach of the South China Sea, which was sponsored by the DaNang Chapel program. Don and I had gone off together looking for wood for a campfire to roast our hot dogs. As we went, we were singing together this song: "I just keep trusting my Lord, as I walk along. I just keep trusting my Lord, as He gives a song. . ."

The last line of the verse of that song is, "I just keep trusting my Lord, He will never fail."

As we sang that song, I put my arm around Don's shoulders, and he did the same to me. We were buddies in love with Jesus. That's when the Lord told Don what to do to teach me the lesson I needed to learn. On the last line of this verse, right when I had my mouth open very wide to sing the word "fail," Don intentionally tripped me. I went face first into the sand, eyes and mouth wide open, with no way of getting my hands in front of me in time to brace my fall.

It was an automatic reaction to jump up swinging at Don, because that was how I was programmed to react to a situation like that before I gave my life to Christ. However, right before I connected my fist with his face, I remembered that I didn't have to obey my flesh anymore, so I stopped myself from following through with my punch, long enough to ask him, screaming, "Why did you do that?"

He simply responded, "So you will learn that I can and will let you down at some point in our relationship. But Jesus will never fail you. You need to get your eyes back on Him and off of me!" Don said to me sternly.

The way the world and my flesh had programmed me to react when someone did something to hurt me was to hurt the person back. But the Spirit of God had already begun reprogramming me to respond differently to adversity, according to God's way of thinking. I wasn't totally reprogrammed at that time, but at least enough change had taken place in me so I didn't kill or hurt Don.

Was I saved at that time? Of course, I was. My spirit was saved. Were my mind and emotions renewed at that time? They were slightly renewed but not nearly as much as they are now after God has taught me for more than forty years. Let's just say, I never consider hurting people as an option as long as I'm listening to the Spirit. However, even now, if I allow the old program to run, I can struggle with unforgiveness and bitterness and a desire to get even.

The way God reprograms our soul is by His Spirit living on the inside of us, which teaches us all spiritual truths. He also uses the written word of truth—the Bible—which has a cleansing effect on our soul.

> *That he might sanctify and cleanse it with the washing of*
> *water by the word, Ephesians 5:26 KJV*

The reprogramming of our soul needs to continue as long as we are on this earth. Unfortunately, the old program never seems to get totally erased, and the new program simply gets added to the hard drive. This makes it important for us to always allow the Spirit to have the preeminent place in our lives or else we can slip back into obeying the flesh quite easily. But we have the promise from God that He will never stop helping us reprogram our soul as long as we are on this earth.

> *Being confident of this very thing, that he which hath*
> *begun a good work in you will perform it until the day of*
> *Jesus Christ: Philippians 1:6 KJV*

The day of Jesus Christ is the day of His return to Earth to gather His children, or bride, to Himself.

> *Let not your heart be troubled: ye believe in God, believe*
> *also in me. In my Father's house are many mansions: if*
> *it were not so, I would have told you. I go to prepare a*
> *place for you. And if I go and prepare a place for you, I*
> *will come again, and receive you unto myself; that where*
> *I am, there ye may be also. John 14:1–3 KJV*

Now, we have seen how our soul must go through a process of salvation or deliverance as long as we are alive on this earth. That is what Paul was referring to in this scripture:

> *Wherefore, my beloved, as ye have always obeyed, not as*
> *in my presence only, but now much more in my absence,*
> *work out your own salvation with fear and trembling. For*
> *it is God which worketh in you both to will and to do of*
> *his good pleasure. Philippians 2:12–13 KJV*

There comes a time in every disciple's life when he or she must become responsible for obeying the Spirit and the Word of God on his or her own. In this scripture, we see Paul reminding the Philippians that he would not be with them any longer to make sure they are allowing their minds to be renewed by the Spirit. This responsibility is now theirs to do with "fear and trembling," because it is a very serious matter. It is a life-and-death situation.

The Spirit Is Our Teacher

Remember how we identified the three parts of our being as spirit, soul, and body. Remember also how we discovered that at the moment we make Jesus Lord of our lives, He gives us the Holy Spirit to live inside us, which means our spirit is completely, 100 percent saved. Please also remember that our soul is not yet delivered or saved—it must undergo the process of deliverance as long as we are on this earth. This process is called the "renewing of our mind,"[24] which is accomplished by the "washing of water by the word."[25] Yet no scripture is to be interpreted by our flesh.[26]

According to the Bible, there is only one who should interpret the scriptures and teach us with it. That is the Holy Spirit, the author Himself.

> *But the Comforter, which is the Holy Ghost, whom the Father will send in my name, he shall teach you all things, and bring all things to your remembrance, whatsoever I have said unto you. John 14:26 KJV*

What the Spirit of God will teach us is *all* things spiritual, because God is Spirit. The Holy Spirit is also called the "Anointing" in this scripture.

> *But the anointing which ye have received of him abideth in you, and ye need not that any man teach you: but as the same anointing teacheth you of all things, and is truth, and*

---

[24] Rom. 12:2.
[25] Eph. 5:26.
[26] 2 Pet. 1:20–21.

is no lie, and even as it hath taught you, ye shall abide in him. 1 John 2:27 KJV

At the time of salvation, the Holy Spirit comes to live inside us, in our spirit. Once He is there, He begins to teach us all things pertaining to the Spirit. We don't need anyone else to teach us, because there is no one else who can teach us spiritual things. What the Spirit teaches us is "truth." Since the Word of God is also called the "truth," then the Spirit and the Word will always agree and confirm one another. In other words, the Spirit will never lead us to do something that the Word of God will not confirm and vice versa. To the degree that we allow the Anointing to teach us the truth, we will abide in Him.

The difference between the Spirit being in us and us being in Him is what we have learned from Him. Christ in us is the hope of our soul and body being saved. Without Him, there's no hope of salvation. We abide in Him to the same degree that He has taught us.

> *. . . and even as It (He) hath taught you, ye shall abide in him. 1 John 2:27 KJV*

After almost a year of being taught by the Spirit, I still cocked my fist when Don intentionally tripped me. Now, after forty years of the Spirit teaching me, I can't even remember the last time I cocked my fist. That response is so foreign to my nature now. To the degree that I have been taught by Him, I abide in Him, or in His nature.

> *Therefore **if** any man be **in** Christ, he is a new creature: old things are passed away; behold, all things are become new. And all things are of God, who hath reconciled us to himself by Jesus Christ, 2 Corinthians 5:17–18 KJV*

The biggest word in the English language is "if." In this scripture the word "if" equals the 1 John 2:27 phrase "as it (He) hath taught you." To the degree that the Holy Spirit has taught us, that is the degree we abide *in* Him. And if we abide in Him, even our body (creature) changes from obeying its own desires and lusts to obeying the Spirit of God. To the degree then that we have been taught of the Holy Spirit, old things have passed away, and in those areas all things have become new.

A Christian's Body Is Waiting to be Delivered

Although our body can be brought under the Spirit's subjection through a soul abiding in Christ, our bodies will not be redeemed in their present state.

> *Because the creature (human body) itself also <u>shall be delivered</u> from the bondage of corruption into the glorious liberty of the children of God. For we know that the whole creation groaneth and travaileth in pain together until now. And not only they, but ourselves also, which have the firstfruits of the Spirit, even we ourselves groan within ourselves, waiting for* **the adoption**, *to wit, the redemption of our body. Romans 8:21–23 KJV, emphasis added*

When Adam and Eve sinned, not only did they experience the curse of that sin but also all the rest of God's creation became partakers of that curse. Before sin, there were no thorns. Before sin there was no disease or destruction. Because of man's sin, all of God's creation is under a curse, waiting to be set free so that it can once again worship God by its existence without being impeded by the pain of this curse.

> *And unto Adam he said, Because thou hast hearkened unto the voice of thy wife, and hast eaten of the tree, of which I commanded thee, saying, Thou shalt not eat of it: cursed is the ground (earth) for thy sake; in sorrow shalt thou eat of it all the days of thy life; Thorns also and thistles shall it bring forth to thee; and thou shalt eat the herb of the field; In the sweat of thy face shalt thou eat bread, till thou return unto the ground; for out of it wast thou taken: for dust thou art, and unto dust shalt thou return. Genesis 3:17–19 KJV*

All of creation waits for the day God calls "the adoption," when all of it, along with our bodies, will be delivered from the curse of sin and redeemed by God. After all, our body is one third of our being, and we have been purchased in our entirety (spirit, soul, and body) by the blood of Jesus. Therefore, Jesus is not about to leave part of His possession behind. He will redeem all of us; and in doing so, He will redeem the rest of his natural creation as well.

> *Beloved, now are we the sons of God, and it doth not yet appear what we shall be: but we know that, when he shall appear, we shall be like him; for we shall see him as he is. 1 John 3:2 KJV*

Because God has given us the down payment toward our total salvation (the earnest of His Spirit), we are considered His children even while we are on earth. In other words, we are as good as "in," because the salvation of our soul and body is not dependent upon us but on Christ. He will perform the work in our soul until He returns to redeem our body as well (Philippians. 1:6). It is a done deal—we are His children. However, right now we have no idea how our body will change when He appears to redeem our body. But one thing we do know is that our bodies will be like His body.

> *For our conversation is in heaven; from whence also we look for the Savior, the Lord Jesus Christ: Who shall change our vile body, that it may be fashioned like unto his glorious body, according to the working whereby he is able even to subdue all things unto himself. Philippians 3:20–21 KJV*

> *Behold, I shew you a mystery; We shall not all sleep (die), but we shall all be changed, in a moment, in the twinkling of an eye, at the last trump: for the trumpet shall sound, and the dead shall be raised incorruptible, and we shall be changed. For this corruptible must put on incorruption, and this mortal must put on immortality.*

So when this corruptible shall have put on incorruption, and this mortal shall have put on immortality, then shall be brought to pass the saying that is written, Death is swallowed up in victory. O death, where is thy sting? O grave, where is thy victory? The sting of death is sin; and the strength of sin is the law. But thanks be to God, which giveth us the victory through our Lord Jesus Christ. 1 Corinthians 15:51–57 KJV

In conclusion, our body is waiting for the day of adoption, the redemption of our body, in which day our body will be changed to be like God's body.

The Three Tenses of Salvation's Deliverance

We have seen that Jesus purchased our entire being on the cross of Calvary. Our Spirit has been saved or delivered, our soul is undergoing the process of salvation, and our body is waiting for the day when it will be changed so it can be saved.

Let's review this again. Our spirit has been (past tense) saved or delivered. Our soul is undergoing (present tense) the deliverance work of salvation. Our body is waiting for the day (future tense) when it will be delivered.

But we had the sentence of death in ourselves, that we should not trust in ourselves, but in God which raiseth the dead: Who delivered us from so great a death, and doth deliver: in whom we trust that he will yet deliver us; 2 Corinthians 1:9–10 KJV

God is the righteous judge sitting in judgment over His creation. When Adam and Eve sinned, God sentenced us all to death on all three levels of our being. The reason He did that, Paul tells us, is so we would not get the mistaken idea that we can trust in ourselves to deliver ourselves from the curse of sin. He wanted us to learn to trust in Christ, who is the only one capable of raising the dead. Through Jesus, all three parts of our being are purchased back to Himself. Our spirit has been delivered. Our soul/mind is being delivered in this present age. Finally, our bodies will be delivered in the future, at the day of adoption. All three parts of our being are provided for in God's redemption plan.

The Worshiper's Anthropology Chart #6

Bible Reference	The Parts of a Human Being		
1 Thessalonians 5:23	spirit	soul	body
Genesis 2:7	breath	soul	form/dust
1 John 5:8	spirit	blood	water
Deuteronomy 6:5	heart	soul	might
2 Corinthians 1:10	delivered	doth deliver	will yet deliver

Table XI

Chapter 4

Becoming Aware of Our Three Parts

Discerning Our Spirit

Most of humanity does not think of themselves as having three parts. We are only "body and soul" to the world's scientific community. These natural, unsaved, or undelivered parts of our being are discernable with our natural mind, but to discern the spirit part of our being requires the Holy Spirit's aid.

> Now we have received, not the spirit of the world, but the spirit which is of God; that we might know the things that are freely given to us of God. Which things also we speak, not in the words which man's wisdom teacheth, but which the Holy Ghost teacheth; comparing spiritual things with spiritual. But the natural man receiveth not the things of the Spirit of God: for they are foolishness unto him: neither can he know them, because they are spiritually discerned. 1 Corinthians 2:12–14 KJV

How does the Holy Spirit teach us to discern the spirit part of our being? As a developing worshiper, we must become aware of each of our three parts, so that we are able to understand what each of these parts does in worship. Fortunately, there is a simple way God teaches us to become aware of our spirit. It is the Word of God.

For the word of God is quick, and powerful, and sharper than any two-edged sword, piercing even to the dividing asunder of soul and spirit, and of the joints and marrow, and is a discerner of the thoughts and intents of the heart. Hebrews 4:12 KJV

I use mostly the King James version (KJV) of the Bible in my writings, because that's all I had to read when I was first saved. I do at times use other versions of the scripture. One reason some people do not like the KJV is because it uses many words that have died out over the years. Some words have not died, but their meaning has been completely changed. One such word in this scripture is "quick." In today's English language, the word "quick" is a synonym of the words "fast" or "speedy." However, at the time the KJV Bible was being translated, synonyms for "quick" would have been "alive" or "living." This is also verified in this scripture:

*I charge thee therefore before God, and the Lord Jesus Christ, who shall judge the **quick** and the **dead** at his appearing and his kingdom; 2 Tim 4:1 KJV, emphasis added*

In Hebrews 4:12, the writer is telling us that the Word of God is alive. The Word of God is made alive by the Spirit of God. Here's how Jesus said it:

It is the spirit that quickeneth; the flesh profiteth nothing: the words that I speak unto you, they are spirit, and they are life. John 6:63 KJV

The Word of God is more than just letters on a page. It is life itself to the followers of Jesus. It is also powerful, and sharper than a two-edged sword. What is the purpose for these three qualities of the word of God? We are told the answer to this in the second part of the scripture.

*. . . piercing even to the **<u>dividing asunder</u>** of <u>soul</u> and <u>spirit</u>, and of the <u>joints and marrow</u>, and is a discerner of*

the thoughts and intents of the heart. Hebrews 4:12b KJV,
emphasis added

The words "joints and marrow" represent the physical part of
our being, because they are the skeletal system, on which our flesh is
attached. Notice in Hebrews 4:12 where the sword pierces and divides
first: our spirit and soul.

The Worshiper's Anthropology Chart #7

Bible Reference	The Parts of a Human Being		
1 Thessalonians 5:23	spirit	soul	body
Genesis 2:7	breath	soul	form/dust
1 John 5:8	spirit	blood	water
Deuteronomy 6:5	heart	soul	might
2 Corinthians 1:10	delivered	doth deliver	will yet deliver
Hebrews 4:12	spirit	soul	Joints & marrow

Table XII

It really does not take spiritual discernment to become aware of the
division between our body and soul. All it takes is natural discernment,
which comes from living life in the flesh. Because of this, God—through
the writer of Hebrews—mentioned the soul/spirit division first in
Hebrews 4:12. He then went on to underline this division by stating "...
and is a discerner of the thoughts and intents of the heart." In studying
what is meant by the "heart," we find that both Strong's[27] and Vine's[28]
define this Greek word this way:

> *[Strong's Greek Number 2588, Greek word: kardia kar-*
> *dee'-ah, Root: prolonged from a primary kar (Latin, cor,*

27 Strong, *Strong's Concordance.*
28 *Vine's Complete Expository Dictionary.*

"heart"), Part of Speech: n f, Usage Notes: KJV - heart 159 times, Simplified definition: 1) denotes the center of all physical or spiritual life, 2a) the vigor and sense of physical life, 2b) the center and seat of spiritual life].[29]

According to this definition, the word "heart" can either refer to our physical heart or our spiritual "heart." Our physical heart is central to our physical lives because, when our heart does not work, there is no physical life. Other organs can fail, and physical life can be sustained for a short time. However, when the heart stops beating, our body stops living.

Hebrews 4:12 is clearly talking about something different from our physical heart. This heart can have both thoughts and intents, which is impossible for the human physical heart to have. Our spiritual heart is the center of our "spiritual life," which is our spirit. The human spirit can have both thoughts and intents. Therefore, we conclude quite easily that the heart that the Word of God helps us to discern is our spirit.

The Word of God is the sword that makes it possible to discern the division between our soul and our spirit. The degree to which we spend time in the Word of God is the degree to which we are able to discern the difference between our soul and our spirit. The less time we spend in the Word of God, the muddier these divisions become to us. This makes it more difficult, if not impossible, to then accomplish the purpose for which we were created.

The Mind Interprets the Leading of the Spirit

All understanding is accomplished by or in our mind. This includes both natural understanding and the understanding of spiritual truths. Human maturity or growth is measured by the level of understanding we have obtained in this life. When God speaks something by His Spirit to our spirit, it is unfruitful to us unless we understand it with our mind.

---

[29] *Vine's Complete Expository Dictionary.*

If then I do not grasp the meaning of what someone is saying, I am a foreigner to the speaker, and he is a foreigner to me. 1 Corinthians 14:11 NIV

God may be speaking to our spirit, but unless He helps us understand what He is saying with our mind, His communication is useless to us. The trouble is that our mind—the major portion of our soul—is still part of the unredeemed portion of our being.

There are three beings who have access to our soul. The first is us. Our soul was given to us to learn, think, feel, and decide. These tasks are accomplished with our mind, emotions, and will.

The physical world has programmed our soul to obey our body since the day we were conceived. Unless we reprogram our soul by the Word of God, we would never recognize when the Spirit of God is speaking to us.

The Holy Spirit is the second person who has access to our mind. We must judge everything God's Spirit leads us to do by the Word of God. The Holy Spirit will never tell us something that will not be validated by the Word of God!

For as many as are led by the Spirit of God, they are the sons of God. Romans 8:14 KJV

The third persons who have access to our souls is the devil and his demons. The reason he has access to our soul is because our soul is part of our being which has not been delivered yet. Satan has access to our minds and emotions; therefore, we must judge every feeling, conclusion, imagination, and thought we have by the Word of God!

Casting down imaginations, and every high thing that exalteth itself against the knowledge of God, and bringing into captivity every thought to the obedience of Christ; 2 Corinthians 10:5 KJV

People who have not spent time in the Word of God are unable to discern the difference between a thought in their mind from God or one from the devil or themselves. People who do not spend time in the Word of God are unable to discern the difference between their own emotions, the passion of the Holy Spirit, and the feelings Satan uses to enslave us.

The church is crowded with Christians who have believed lies from the enemy as truth from God, because they have not spent time reading the Word of God for themselves. Hearing the Word read to us for five minutes each week is simply not adequate.

Two Biblical Swords

In Hebrews 4:12, the Word of God is said to be a two-edged sword that is God's way of teaching us how to discern the spirit part of our being. In other words, the more we read the Bible, the more we learn the way God talks and the kind of things He will say to us. That way, when He speaks to us by His Spirit, we recognize it right away.

This also allows us to recognize when Satan is trying to deceive us with a half-truth. By the way, Satan never starts out telling us a total lie. He couches his lies in truth in hopes we will accept the whole thought as truth. The Word of God helps us recognize which thoughts are truth and which are lies. Once we have recognized a lie, the other edge of the sword/Word of God is used as an offensive weapon against Satan.

> *And take the helmet of salvation, and the sword of the Spirit, which is the word of God: Ephesians 6:17 KJV*

Jesus demonstrated for us how to use this sword against the devil when He was tempted in the desert, as described in Matthew 4:1–11. Also, Satan demonstrated in this same narrative how he takes truth out of context to tempt with a half-truth.

There is another Biblical sword that we discussed briefly in the book *Biblical Worship*. It, too, is a very effective offensive weapon against the enemy when used correctly. It is the spiritual sword of high praises.

> *Let the high praises of God be in their mouth, and (which is) a two-edged sword in their hand, Psalm 149:6 NKJV*

Biblically, high praise and the Word of God are both considered as spiritual swords! Please make note that a sword is an offensive weapon first, yet it is also used defensively in natural swordplay. The Word of God and our worship of God are both for spiritual offense and defense.

Being Led by the Spirit

After we become a Christian, we are expected to be always led by the Spirit.

> *For as many as are led by the Spirit of God, these are sons of God. Romans 8:14 NKJV*

To be led by God's Spirit is not to be led by some external force. Remember, God places His Spirit within man, so we feel Him leading us from within. When we give ourselves to the Lordship of Jesus, His Spirit comes to live on the inside of us and joins Himself to our spirit. Therefore, for a Christian to be led by the spirit is to be led by the Holy Spirit, who is now joined to our spirit.

Every breath we breathe, every turn we take, every word we speak, everything we do, every purchase we make, everything is to be led by the Spirit. We are not our own, we have been purchased by the blood of Jesus. God now owns us, and He wants to direct every step we take, just as He directed Jesus when He was in the flesh.

> *Then answered Jesus and said unto them, Verily, verily, I say unto you, The Son can do nothing of himself, but what he seeth the Father do: for what things soever he doeth, these also doeth the Son likewise. John 5:19 KJV*

> *For I have not spoken of myself; but the Father which sent me, he gave me a commandment, what I should say, and what I should speak. And I know that his commandment is life everlasting: whatsoever I speak therefore, even as the Father said unto me, so I speak. John 12:49–50 KJV*

Everything the Spirit of God directs us to do or say will conform to holiness and righteousness. However, the Bible is full of stories where God led people to do absolutely bizarre things. Many Christians who have not spent much time in the Word of God have been led astray by their own thoughts or thoughts planted in their mind by our enemy. This happens because they did not know how to recognize the leading of the Spirit of God.

The Spirit of God will never lead us to do something that the Bible will not confirm. Without the Bible as our guide, it is impossible to know which things are coming from our spirit, and which are coming from our soul. We must have the sword of the Spirit to reveal truth to us in the "inward parts."[30]

Dividing Ourselves into Two Parts

In the last chapter, we learned that only one-third of our three-part being is saved or delivered: our spirit, which has been joined to God's Spirit. Our soul is being reprogrammed according to the Word of God as long as we are on this earth. Our body must wait for the day of adoption, which is the day our body will be changed. The body and soul, which are the not-yet-redeemed parts of a Christian, make up what the Bible calls "the flesh."

> *There is therefore now no condemnation to them which are in Christ Jesus, who walk (live) not after the flesh, but after the Spirit. Romans 8:1 KJV*

If we want to consider ourselves as a two-part being, we need to divide ourselves where the scriptures divide us—between the soul and spirit, between the redeemed part of us and the not-yet-redeemed parts. Notice that if we live our lives obeying the desires of our "flesh" instead of our "spirit," the end result will be "condemnation."

The KJV Bible also uses a unique word to describe someone who

---

[30] Ps. 51:6.

is not developing spiritually, who is still obeying the influences of their flesh.

> *And I, brethren, could not speak unto you as unto*
> *spiritual, but as unto carnal, even as unto babes in Christ.*
> *1 Corinthians 3:1 KJV*

The result of living our lives as slaves to our flesh or carnally is very severe: We will not grow or develop into spiritual maturity. Yet, the results of living our lives under the influence of God's Spirit are very rewarding.

> *For they that are after the flesh do mind the things of*
> *the flesh; but they that are after the Spirit the things of*
> *the Spirit. For to be carnally minded is death; but to be*
> *spiritually minded is life and peace. Because the carnal*
> *mind is enmity against God: for it is not subject to the law*
> *of God, neither indeed can be. So then they that are in the*
> *flesh cannot please God. Romans 8:5–8 KJV*

Please notice how our "mind" (part of our soul) can be controlled or influenced by either our flesh or our spirit. If we allow our mind to develop in a carnal way, the end result is death. If we allow our mind to develop under the influence of the Spirit and the Word of God, we will find true life and peace.

Spiritual Development

For the unsaved to be spiritually minded, at best, will be no different from being carnally minded, which will produce the same result—death. However, it is possible to develop spiritually before our spirit is regenerated by the Holy Spirit. This type of spiritual development opens us up to all types of demonic spiritual influences. Such "spiritual" development is never healthy and will always result in humans becoming a long-term slave of the demons they have opened themselves up to.

Our common ancestors, Adam and Eve, disobeyed God's instructions and suffered a punishment for their actions—separation from God on all three levels of their being. Adam and Eve's spirits died immediately when they were cut off from God's presence. This meant Adam's soul no longer had a Godly spiritual influence upon it, so Adam's soul deteriorated into being carnal or fleshly. And, of course, Adam's body eventually died as well. This is how mankind experienced death on all three levels of our being. Every human being is born after the state of our ancestors Adam and Eve—spiritually dead, dying physically, and developing in our soul according to all this death.

I'm a visual learner, so it helps me to understand when I can see things in a chart.

Adam & Eve's Death on Three Levels

spirit	soul	body
Immediate death	Developing death	Eventual death

Our Salvation on Three Levels

spirit	soul	body
Immediately saved	Salvation process	Eventual redemption

Table XIII

Once our spirit has been made alive by being joined to God's Spirit, then we can begin to change who we are by putting off who we were and putting on who we are becoming.

> *That ye put off concerning the former conversation (way of life) the old man, which is corrupt according to the deceitful lusts (of the flesh); and be renewed in the spirit (NIV says "attitude") of your mind; and that ye put on the new man, which after God is created in righteousness and true holiness. Ephesians 4:22–24 KJV*

The new man is made after the Spirit, the old man is made after the flesh. The old man is who we are when we are first joined to God's

Spirit. The new man is who we will become if we allow the Spirit of God and Word of God to lead us for the rest of our earthly lives. The earth is where we are undergoing the change into a new man in our soul.

In other words, until our soul is renewed by the Word of God and the Spirit of God, the unregenerated soul and dying body are considered "the old man." It is also called the "natural man" in this scripture.

> But the natural man receiveth not the things of the Spirit of God: for they are foolishness unto him: neither can he know them, because they are spiritually discerned. 1 Corinthians 2:14 KJV

Notice the words "know them," and remember that, as human beings, we develop and grow naturally through natural knowledge. Likewise, we grow spiritually through spiritual knowledge.

Remember that at the time of creation, mankind was the only creature that God had to teach about eating.[31] All the other creatures God had preprogrammed to eat according to the food chain He designed. Now we teach our offspring how to eat. God ordained that human beings will develop or grow by gaining knowledge or understanding. Animals develop different behaviors only if a human teaches them something to be done on command. God created us to grow by understanding the reason for behavior change, not just the command.

Here is another way God described the division between our natural man and our spiritual man.

> What is the conclusion then? I will pray with the spirit, and I will also pray with the understanding. I will sing with the spirit, and I will also sing with the understanding. 1 Corinthians 14:15 NKJV

Now we are at the place in our study where we can add these scriptures about the duality of mankind to our Anthropology Chart.

---

[31] Ge. 1:29

The Worshiper's Anthropology Chart #8

Bible Reference	The Parts of a Human Being		
1 Thessalonians 5:23	spirit	soul	body
Genesis 2:7	breath	soul	form/dust
1 John 5:8	spirit	blood	water
Deuteronomy 6:5	heart	soul	might
2 Corinthians 1:10	delivered	doth deliver	will yet deliver
Hebrews 4:12	spirit	soul	Joints & marrow
Romans 8:1	spirit	flesh	
1 Corinthians 3:1	spiritual	carnal	
Ephesians 4:22–24	new man	old man	
1 Corinthians 2:14	spirit	natural man	
1 Corinthians 14:15	spirit	understanding	

Table XIV

Gaining Understanding

This is how natural understanding works, how it is obtained, and how it is retained. The first step of gaining natural understanding is to receive data through your five senses—seeing, hearing, smelling, tasting, and touching. Information comes into our soul from our five senses as raw data.

To gain understanding requires that our soul process this data. Conclusions regarding this data involve the three parts of our soul. We have gained understanding when we answer these three questions:

1. What do we know and think about this data? (mind)
2. How do we feel about this data? (emotions)

3. What will we do about these conclusions? (will)

These conclusions and subsequent actions—along with any supporting, relevant data—are then stored in our memory as natural understanding. When accessing this memory in the future, we will only review this event based on our conclusions, actions, and supporting data. Our minds don't need to reopen the raw data of that memory once we have reached these conclusions. People who continually relive or recall raw data memories tend to become psychiatrically or emotionally unstable.

The Function of Our Parts in Worship

We know we were created for the purpose of worshiping our Creator; therefore, the design of our being allows us to fulfill that purpose. The question remains—how do we worship God with all three parts of our being?

For the rest of this book, we will examine each of the three parts of our being and discover biblically how each part is to function in the expression of our worship to Almighty God.

Remember, worship is the expression of love from mankind to God. In the book *Biblical Worship*, I showed you in scripture how worship is forbidden to be directed toward anyone but God.

Let me give you a preview of what is to come by showing you our completed anthropology chart. The words in the final three lines of the chart do not appear anywhere in scriptures, but rather I have summarized the concepts of the scripture references given in the chart into these last three words. We will take the time to study each of these scriptures when we study each part's function in worship.

The Worshiper's Anthropology Chart #9

Bible Reference	The Parts of a Human Being		
1 Thessalonians 5:23	spirit	soul	body
Genesis 2:7	breath	soul	form/dust
1 John 5:8	spirit	blood	water
Deuteronomy 6:5	heart	soul	might
2 Corinthians 1:10	delivered	doth deliver	will yet deliver
Hebrews 4:12	spirit	soul	joints & marrow
Romans 8:1	spirit	flesh	
1 Corinthians 3:1	spiritual	carnal	
Ephesians 4:22–24	new man	old man	
1 Corinthians 2:14	spirit	natural man	
1 Corinthians 14:15	spirit	understanding	
Bible Reference	**The Responsibility of our Parts in Worship**		
1 Corinthians 12:3	initiator		
Romans 10:9–10			expresser
Romans 12:2		conductor	

Table XV

Chapter 5

The Spirit's Function in Worship

The Spirit Initiates Everything Spiritual

Without God's Spirit joined to our spirit, we would never initiate or pursue a relationship with God.

> *As it is written, There is none righteous, no, not one: There is none that understandeth, there is none that seeketh after God. They are all gone out of the way, they are together become unprofitable; there is none that doeth good, no, not one. Romans 3:10–12 KJV*

Here is the scripture Paul was referring to in the Old Testament:

> *God looked down from heaven upon the children of men, to see if there were any that did understand, that did seek God. Every one of them is gone back: they are altogether become filthy; there is none that doeth good, no, not one. Psalms 53:2–3 KJV*

Left in our unredeemed state, none of us would ever seek after God, to be a worshiper of Him. That would be foreign to us, something we would never do. No one ever pursues a relationship with their enemy, therefore it was left entirely up to God to pursue a relationship with us.

All we like sheep have gone astray; we have turned everyone to his own way; and the LORD hath laid on him (Jesus) the iniquity of us all. Isaiah 53:6 KJV

And there is none that calleth upon thy name, that stirreth up himself to take hold of thee: for thou hast hid thy face from us, and hast consumed us, because of our iniquities. But now, O LORD, thou art our father; we are the clay, and thou our potter; and we all are the work of thy hand. Isaiah 64:7–8 KJV

Ye have not chosen me, but I have chosen you, and ordained you, that ye should go and bring forth fruit, and that your fruit should remain: that whatsoever ye shall ask of the Father in my name, he may give it you. John 15:16 KJV

We did not choose God—He chose us. We did not stir up ourselves to take hold of God. He pursued us. He stirred us up to desire Him. He initiated our relationship with Him, and He initiates the continuation of our relationship with Him. He is the initiator in this love relationship; we are the responders. That's why we are called His bride, not His husband. For as the man is the normal initiator in the expression of love in the marriage act, so is God's Spirit in our relationship with Him.

Yet, not only does God initiate a love relationship between us and Himself, but God also gives us the love to give back to Him in our relationship with Him. All that we give to God is first given to us by God to give back to Him. Notice how in a time of worship David received this very important revelation.

Now therefore, our God, we thank thee, and praise thy glorious name. But who am I, and what is my people, that we should be able to offer so willingly after this sort? for all things come of thee, and of thine own have we given thee. 1 Chronicles 29:13–14 KJV

In the New Testament, John received the same revelation, and wrote it down in this way:

And they came unto John, and said unto him, Rabbi, he that was with thee beyond Jordan, to whom thou barest witness, behold, the same baptizeth, and all men come to him. John answered and said, A man can receive nothing, except it be given him from heaven. John 3:26–27 KJV

God has stirred us up to seek Him, to love Him, to worship Him; and by His Spirit, God has provided the love for us to give back to Him. Why did God do things this way? Here is God's answer to that question.

For God, who commanded the light to shine out of darkness, hath shined in our hearts, to give the light of the knowledge of the glory of God in the face of Jesus Christ. But we have this treasure in earthen vessels, that the excellency of the power may be of God, and not of us. 2 Corinthians 4:6–7 KJV

God wanted everything about our relationship with Him to be "of" Him and not of us. We have His Spirit resident within our "earthen vessel," which is our body, so that His initiation of our relationship with him and the expression of our love to Him might all come from Him and not from us.

The Declaration of Our Worship Relationship

To declare that Jesus is our Lord qualifies us to be one of His worshipers. Look at this list of relationships between God and man, which is from the book *Biblical Worship*.

Biblical Relationships with God

God	us
Creator	creation
Deity	humanity
Savior	sinner
Teacher	student
King	subject

Lord	servant
Master	bond-slave
Strong One	weak one
Independent	dependent
Friend	friend
Father	son/child
Bridegroom	bride

Table XVI

This may not be an exhaustive list, but it serves the purpose of showing that we have many different biblical ways of relating to God.

We also discovered in Chapter Four of *Biblical Worship* that it is not scriptural to worship peers or equals. Worship is reserved for expressing mankind's love to the Almighty God, never to any created beings. In other words, a worship relationship between God and man requires that God be exalted and man be abased.

The first relationship we declare and enter into with God, once we have realized we are sinners and that Jesus is our only Savior, is when we make Jesus Lord of our lives. This is how the salvation process begins for all of us, and this is what qualifies us to be a worshiper of Jesus.

> *That if thou shalt confess with thy mouth the **Lord** Jesus, and shalt believe in thine heart that God hath raised him from the dead, thou shalt be saved. Romans 10:9 KJV, emphasis added*

Notice that we do not declare Jesus is our Savior to get saved. We must declare that Jesus is Lord to start the salvation process and to qualify ourselves to be a worshiper of Jesus. To do this is not a small thing. It requires a supernatural prompting of the Holy Spirit to declare that Jesus is Lord of our lives.

> *Therefore I make known to you that no one speaking by the Spirit of God calls Jesus accursed, and no one can say that Jesus is Lord except by the Holy Spirit. 1 Corinthians 12:3 NKJV*

You may be able to say the words "Jesus is Lord" with your lips and not mean them, but when it comes down to the test, no one can declare the Lordship of Jesus without the Spirit of God prompting him or her to do so.

More than thirty years ago, I heard a story about a Christian missionary who was in India. I believe it is a true story, however, I am unable to document this story with names, dates, and places. I heard the story from a speaker on a cassette tape recorded at a missionaries' gathering. This is the story as I remember it.

God had used the missionary to bring many Muslims to Jesus in India. Of course, other Muslims hated him for that and sought to discredit him publicly, because their attempts to kill him had all failed.

As was their custom, several of the Christian missionaries in India were flying into a major city to meet together for encouragement, which they did two or three times each year.

As the missionary deplaned and entered the airport, a couple of Muslim leaders recognized him. These Muslims followed him to the baggage claim area, so there would be a maximum number of people standing around. In front of hundreds of people, the educated Muslim's loudly addressed the Christian.

"Hey," one shouted, "you're that Christian, aren't you?

"I am a Christian," the missionary responded.

"Well, doesn't your Bible say that no one can say Jesus is Lord except by the Spirit of God?"

"Yes, it does," the missionary responded.

"Well, Jesus is lord," the Muslim said very sarcastically. "So how do you respond to that?"

Chuckles could be heard throughout the crowd, and a big smile came across the faces of the Muslims. They were confident the missionary would not be able to explain this away.

The missionary was red in the face from embarrassment. He had no idea how to respond to this mockery of his faith.

About that time, a group of Christian missionaries, who were in India to attend the missionaries' conference, were approaching the baggage claim area. At that moment, the Spirit of the Lord told the missionary what to do.

Raising his voice and placing his cupped hand close to his mouth, he shouted down the corridor, "Hey brothers, come here! These Muslims are saying that Jesus is Lord!"

Before the group of missionaries could get to where their friend was, the Muslims had turned and ran away. No one in the crowd could make eye contact with any of the missionaries.

It is possible to say things with our mouth that we don't believe in our heart. That's why we confess with our mouth and believe in our heart to start the salvation process.

Do you remember the girl who was killed for her declaration of faith at the Columbine High School in Denver, Colorado? She was asked by the gunman, "Do you believe in Jesus Christ?"

Her quick response, without hesitation, was, "Yes I do!" And those were the last words she spoke on this earth.

How was she able to do that? Would we do that if we found ourselves in the same situation? Left to ourselves, we will fail this test every time. However, when Jesus lives on the inside of us and His Spirit is joined to our spirit, there is no doubt that we will—by the Holy Ghost—declare boldly that Jesus is our Lord!

The Spirit Initiates Our Worship

To declare that Jesus is Lord is itself an act of worship. The Spirit of God initiates our love relationship with Jesus, and He also initiates the expression of our love to Jesus, which is worship. Let me remind you of our anthropology chart for this point.

The Worshiper's Anthropology Chart #10

Bible Reference	The Responsibility of our Parts in Worship		
1 Thessalonians 5:23	spirit	soul	body
1 Corinthians 12:3	initiator		

Table XVII

Therefore, the Spirit of God on the inside of us will initiate *all* worship. Worship that is initiated any other way, or from any other part of our being, is *not* true, biblical worship!

Thy Will Be Done

God gave mankind free will, which allows us to choose whether we will function according to the Spirit's leading. Therefore, when God's Spirit calls mankind to worship Him, we may or may not respond correctly.

> *I love to do God's will so far as my new nature is concerned; but there is something else deep within me, in my lower nature, that is at war with my (renewed) mind and wins the fight and makes me a slave to the sin that is still within me. In my (renewed) mind I want to be God's willing servant, but instead I find myself still enslaved to sin. So you see how it is: my new life tells me to do right, but the old nature that is still inside me loves to sin. Oh, what a terrible predicament I'm in! Who will free me from my slavery to this deadly lower nature? Thank God! It has been done by Jesus Christ our Lord. Romans 7:22–23 Living*

The reason Christians do not always do exactly what the Spirit of God wants us to do is because our will is part of our soul, which is a part of our being that is not yet redeemed. Because of this, every Christian sometimes makes decisions according to the influence of our flesh, instead of our Spirit, just like Paul talked about in the aforementioned scripture, even though the renewed part of our mind knows it is wrong to do this.

Yet, there is a place where we follow God's will explicitly. That place is heaven. We know this because of the model prayer Jesus used to answer His disciple's request that he teach them to pray.

> *After this manner therefore pray ye: Our Father which art in heaven, Hallowed be thy name. Thy kingdom come. Thy will be done **in earth, as it is in heaven**. Give us this day*

our daily bread. And forgive us our debts, as we forgive our debtors. And lead us not into temptation, but deliver us from evil: For thine is the kingdom, and the power, and the glory, forever. Amen. Matthew 6:9–13 KJV, emphasis added

The reason we should ask God for His will to be done on earth as it is done in heaven is because in heaven God's will is always being done. The only time when God's will was not done in heaven was when Lucifer rebelled against God, wanting worship for himself and wanting to be like God. God immediately purged heaven of this rebellion and restored it to the place where God's will is always being done.

If in heaven God's will is always being done, what then goes on in heaven?

In the year that king Uzziah died I saw also the Lord sitting upon a throne, high and lifted up, and his train filled the temple. Above it stood the seraphims: each one had six wings; with twain he covered his face, and with twain he covered his feet, and with twain he did fly. And one cried unto another, and said, Holy, holy, holy, is the LORD of hosts: the whole earth is full of his glory. Isaiah 6:1–3 KJV

Here is John's report of his visit to heaven, which he wrote about in his written Revelation, the last book of the Bible. This account of a heavenly visit came over seven hundred years after Isaiah's visit to heaven.

And immediately I was in the spirit: and, behold, a throne was set in heaven, and one sat on the throne. And he that sat was to look upon like a jasper and a sardine stone: and there was a rainbow round about the throne, in sight like unto an emerald. And round about the throne were four and twenty seats: and upon the seats I saw four and twenty elders sitting, clothed in white raiment; and they had on their heads crowns of gold. And out of the throne proceeded lightnings and thunderings and voices: and there were seven lamps of fire burning before the throne, which are the seven Spirits of God.

> *And before the throne there was a sea of glass like unto crystal: and in the midst of the throne, and round about the throne, were four beasts full of eyes before and behind. And the first beast was like a lion, and the second beast like a calf, and the third beast had a face as a man, and the fourth beast was like a flying eagle. And the four beasts had each of them six wings about him; and they were full of eyes within: and they rest not day and night, saying, Holy, holy, holy, Lord God Almighty, which was, and is, and is to come Revelation 4:2–8 KJV*

I find it interesting that, although there were seven hundred years between Isaiah's visit to heaven and John's visit to heaven, heaven was still worshipping God with the same song, "Holy, holy, holy. . ." It seems they got in on different verses of the song, but it was still the same song. And to think, I've heard Christians complain about a song in our worship service being sung four or five times. Just wait till we get to heaven and take a thousand years to sing just one song of praise to Jesus. Who will they complain to then? It won't be me, praise God! I will not be the worship leader in heaven.

Not just the ones closest to the thrown in heaven do the worshipping, but everyone there is worshipping Jesus.

> *And I beheld, and I heard the voice of many angels round about the throne and the beasts and the elders: and the number of them was ten thousand times ten thousand, and thousands of thousands; Saying with a loud voice, Worthy is the Lamb that was slain to receive power, and riches, and wisdom, and strength, and honor, and glory, and blessing. Revelation 5:11–12 KJV*

We see from these scriptures that, in heaven, where God's will is being accomplished all the time, the primary activity is worship of the Almighty God and the Lamb of God. This confirms what we already know: that the purpose for all of creation is to worship God. This includes every part of creation, not just the inhabitants of earth.

In heaven, where God's will is being accomplished all the time, we see worship of the Almighty God going on. How often is the Spirit of God initiating worship in heaven? Read this scripture again, slowly, to find out the answer to that question.

> *And the four beasts had each of them six wings about him; and they were full of eyes within: and **they rest not day and night**, saying, Holy holy, holy, Lord God Almighty, which was, and is, and is to come. Revelation 4:8 KJV, emphasis added*

In heaven, worship never ceases! In heaven, where God's will is always being accomplished, worship is taking place "day and night." Therefore, we understand that God's Spirit is always initiating worship from His people, whether they are in heaven or on the earth. The Spirit is continually initiating worship of Jesus in His people's hearts. For us to pray that God's will is done on earth like it is being done in heaven is actually to pray that we, His people, will function in the purpose for which we were created—to worship God twenty-four hours a day, seven days a week.

The Spirit of God Is Always Initiating Worship

Notice this confirmation scripture concerning the fact that the Spirit of God is always compelling us to worship Jesus from the last chapter of the book of Hebrews.

> *By him therefore let us offer the sacrifice of praise to God **continually**, that is, the fruit of our lips giving thanks to his name. Hebrews 13:15 KJV, emphasis added*

How often does it say in this scripture that we are supposed to offer the "sacrifice of praise" to God? We are to offer praise continually, day and night, because that is how often God's Spirit, which is now joined to our spirit, is prompting us to worship the Lord. He never ceases to prompt us to worship Jesus.

The question is what determines whether we obey the Spirit and worship Jesus? It is our will. We must choose to obey the new nature, not the old nature—the Spirit, not the flesh. This is why praise or worship of the Lord is called a "sacrifice." To our flesh and the unrenewed portion of our soul, obeying the Spirit of God's initiation of worship can be a real sacrifice—but one with great rewards and well worth the sacrifice.

Notice in this scripture, Hebrews 13:15, that we do not initiate worship but that praise only happens "by Him." The Spirit is initiating worship "continually," "day and night." It is possible to live in an attitude of worship twenty-four hours a day. It's called "walking after the Spirit." To obey the Spirit of God is to be a worshiper all the time, twenty-four hours a day, seven days a week.

> *Rejoice evermore. Pray without ceasing. In everything give thanks: for this is the will of God in Christ Jesus concerning you. 1 Thessalonians 5:16–18 KJV*

We already know that "rejoice" is a synonym of the word "worship." Through a quick word study, we find that the word "evermore" means "always and forever." Therefore, we are being commanded to worship God all the time, without stopping.

The word "pray" in this scripture is comprised of two Greek words, which mean:

> *". . . to pray (to God)," by "humble(ing) yourselves."*[32]

In other words, prayer is petitioning God as an expression of trust in God. That is trust to the level that allows Him to be our Lord, Father, and Lover. Such an act fulfills the definition of worship and allows us to begin to understand why prayer is the most powerful expression of individual worship that God has given to us. After all, no one would pray to a god whom they did not worship.

"Giving thanks to God" is also the same thing as worshipping God. The words "in everything" also imply both "always and forever." The

---

[32] *Vine's Complete Expository Dictionary.*

word "everything" refers to both everything in the present and also everything in the future.

Worshiping God 24/7

To many, the concept of being a worshiper on a continual basis seems impossible. Yet, we have all of these scriptures instructing us to do so. How do we reconcile this?

There are two keys to accomplish these commandments. The first key to worshipping God continually is for our waking hours. While awake, no matter what we are doing, we should always focus on the Holy Spirit within us, since He always will be initiating worship from us. If we have trouble knowing how to recognize what the Spirit is initiated within us, remember our conclusion of our study on Hebrews 4:12. The degree to which we spend time in God's Word will be the degree to which we will be able to recognize what is coming from the Spirit.

The second key is for the sleeping hours. To understand this key, we need to understand that only our body must sleep to be rejuvenated every day. Our spirit, just like God's Spirit, does not sleep.

> He will not suffer thy foot to be moved: he that keepeth thee will not slumber. Behold, he that keepeth Israel shall neither slumber nor sleep. Psalms 121:3–4 KJV

God is a Spirit,[33] and spirits do not require sleep. Therefore, our spirit, which is joined to God's Spirit within our body, does not require sleep either.

Sleep studies reveal that our brain—the processing center of our soul—is not dormant during sleep either but is constantly active during the sleep cycles.

One of the activities our mind engages in as we sleep is to review every event of our previous day. My friend was the CEO of an organization that uses technology developed at the University of Illinois to teach handicapped children how to ride a two-wheel bicycle. While explaining

---

[33] John 4:24.

how they are able to teach these children how to ride a bicycle in just five days, he explained one sleep function of our mind to me and how they make use of it in their teaching process.

The kids only ride under supervision the specially adapted bicycles for an hour or so each of the five days. They are told to go home and *not* practice on their personal bikes at all. When they sleep at night, their brains will review every activity of the day. If it is a new activity, the brain will review it several times. My friend told me that when the kids come back the next day, they have actually improved in their riding skills from where they were when they went home the day before. Repeating this process for five days and four nights and putting the children on a different technology adapted bicycle each day results in 80 percent of the handicapped children being able to ride a normal bicycle within just five-plus hours of riding on five different days.

When you worship God all your waking hours, your mind will continue those activities of your day while you sleep. The next day it will even be easier to worship God "continually," because you will have been reviewing that activity all night long as you slept.

Therefore, just like our spirit does not need to sleep, neither does our soul. While our body sleeps, our mind is active.[34], [35] Many scientific studies have been conducted concerning how it is possible for our mind to make conscious decisions while our body is sleeping

If a person has worked at being a worshiper during his or her waking hours by keying into the Spirit inside of himself or herself and obeying His lead to express love to Jesus, it will be a natural extension of this habit to continue obeying the Spirit with the soul even while the body sleeps. When this happens, our being will not know the difference between the actual physical expression of worship and reliving the many memory files of our waking hours in worship. As we stay tuned to the Holy Spirit with

[34] "Sleep: A Dynamic Activity," National Institute of Neurological Disorders and Strokes, accessed February 3, 2017, http://www.ninds.nih.gov/disorders/brain_basics/understanding_sleep.htm#dynamic_activity.
[35] "Human Brain Still Awake, Even During Deep Sleep," University of Liège, last modified October 17, 2008, accessed on July 3, 2014, http://www.sciencedaily.com/releases/2008/10/081008101740.htm.

our soul, we will continue to obey His initiation of worship twenty-four hours a day, seven days a week.

Many times I have woken myself up praising God either from my lips or in my mind, as if from my lips. Sometimes I awake reliving a memory file of praising God; and if I stay in tune with the Holy Spirit, it is not long before I begin to worship the Lord audibly with the fruit of my lips.

It is definitely possible for us to get to the place where we are continually offering the sacrifice of praise to God. But more than that, the Lord expects and commands this type of continual worship, day and night, from us! Since He wants this from us, if we give Him a chance, He will bring it to pass in our lives.

Chapter 6

The Body's Function in Worship

Our Spirit Needs Our Body to Express Worship

Each of our three parts are necessary to accomplish true worship. The Spirit, which has been joined to God's Spirit, is the initiator of all true, biblical worship, which we discussed in Chapter Five. However, love is no good unless it is expressed, so God has given man the physical part of our being to be the expresser of what is in our soul or spirit.

God has given our body to us to serve as the expresser of our being. Our spirit and soul need our body to be able to express ourselves on any level—natural or spiritual.

Body Expression Is Required for Salvation

Even from the beginning of a redemptive relationship with the Lord, which most of us call the "salvation experience," we see that it is necessary to involve our body in the expression of our heart to experience spiritual rebirth.

> *But what saith it? The word is nigh thee, even in thy mouth, and in thy heart: that is, the word of faith, which we preach; That if thou shalt confess with thy mouth the Lord Jesus, and shalt believe in thine heart that God hath raised him from the dead, thou shalt be saved. For with*

the heart man believeth unto righteousness; and with the
mouth confession is made unto salvation. For the scripture
saith, Whosoever believeth on him shall not be ashamed.
Romans 10:8–11 KJV

In this classic salvation scripture, we see the necessity of declaring Jesus to be Lord over us. This declaration of His Lordship is the proof that His Spirit has joined itself to our spirit, because no one can call Jesus Lord except by the Spirit of God.

Wherefore I give you to understand, that no man speaking
by the Spirit of God calleth Jesus accursed: and that no
man can say that Jesus is the Lord, but by the Holy Ghost.
1 Corinthians 12:3 KJV

At the moment our spiritual eyes are opened to believe that Jesus, who is God, came to earth in the flesh; lived a sinless life, which qualified Him to be the supreme sacrifice for our sins; was crucified on the cross; and was raised from the dead, we are able to declare the Lord Jesus from our heart with our lips.

For us to begin our walk toward complete salvation, which will be completed at "the day of our Lord," believing the truth of Jesus in our heart *must* be accompanied by the expression of the truth that Jesus is our Lord.

The salvation process doesn't start until we express our heart with our mouth. In every aspect of our spiritual life, what is in our heart must be expressed by our body for it to count. It does not work to say "I worship God in my spirit, so that should be good enough for God." God gave us a body to express ourselves with, and He intends for us to use our body when expressing our love to Him!

A couple had been married for nearly thirty years when they ended up in the marriage counselor's office. "What seems to be the problem?" the counselor asked.

"He doesn't love me!" the woman cried.

"Where'd you get that idea?" her husband asked, bewildered.

"Well, you never tell me you love me," she explained.

"Well, I told you I love you thirty years ago," the man remarked in disbelief, "and if it had changed, don't you think I would have told you?"

A love relationship needs to be expressed continually for it to grow. It's not enough to express love once in a relationship. You must express love every day, many times a day, to be current or up-to-date. Telling God you love him yesterday is not good enough for today.

The brilliant lyricist Oscar Hammerstein II wrote these lyrics as the introduction to the reprise of the song "Sixteen Going On Seventeen."[36]

A bell is no bell till you ring it.

A song is no song till you sing it.

And love in your heart wasn't put there to stay.

Love isn't love till you give it away.

In the same way, worship is never worship until we express it. The spirit cannot worship on its own—it requires the body to express what the spirit initiates.

The Worshiper's Anthropology Chart #11

Bible Reference	The Responsibility of our Parts in Worship		
1 Thessalonians 5:23	spirit	soul	body
1 Corinthians 12:3	initiator		
Romans 10:9–10			expresser

Table XVIII

God Choses Our Expressions of Worship

Is God concerned with how we express our worship to Him? Does God simply want us to express worship to Him in expressions of our own choice?

To answer these questions, let's look again at the story of Cane and Able.

And in the process of time it came to pass that Cain brought an offering of the fruit of the ground to the Lord.

---

[36] Sixteen Going On Seventeen, from the musical "The Sound of Music," Rogers and Hammerstein, published in 1959

Abel also brought of the firstborn of his flock and of their fat. And the Lord respected Abel and his offering, but He did not respect Cain and his offering. And Cain was very angry, and his countenance fell. Genesis 4:3–5 NKJV

Since God rejected Cain's offering of worship, that clearly tells us that there are ways of expressing worship to God that God does not accept. We need to find out what expressions of worship are acceptable to God and which are not. How do we find out which expressions of worship are acceptable to God?

In Jesus' famous discourse on worship to the woman of Samaria, we learn the key to finding out the way God wants to be worshiped. This teaching on worship from Jesus came because a Samaritan woman asked Him a question about worship to distract Him from revealing more of her personal sins. Jesus had already revealed some of her sins by telling her she had been married to five husbands and was living with a sixth man who was not her husband.

Although Jesus knew she was trying to squirm out from under the conviction she was feeling, He simply answered her question in a loving way. His answer, however, was so incredibly profound that we can receive a multitude of revelations about biblical worship by studying His very short teaching.

Jesus Teaches on Worship

The Bible text of this story is found in John 4:1-42. I recommend that you take the time to read it in the scriptures before you read any further in this book.

I have both studied and taught drama at the college level throughout my life. One of the things I have learned is how to read a script or a story and glean the characters' emotions and internal dialog. Please permit me to tell you this story in my own words using this acquired skill.

Jesus' message revealed to the world that He was creator/God come in the flesh to bring the Kingdom of God to mankind.

From the early years of Jesus' ministry, the Pharisees realized that Jesus made and baptized more disciples than John the Baptist, which made Jesus more of a target of their anger than John. To avoid a premature confrontation with them, Jesus left Judaea and departed again into Galilee. As He traveled with His twelve chosen disciples, He told them that He must go through Samaria. Although this was highly unusual for Jews in that day, the disciples did not verbally question Jesus as to why.

There was a long-term hatred between the Jews and the Samaritans. The Samaritans were a cross-bred nation of Jews and Gentiles who were not accepted by either race. The Jews felt the Samaritans were so corrupted as human beings that they even refused to touch a Samaritan. Tradition tells us that when a Jew made a business deal with a Samaritan, the Jew would drape his cloak over his hand before shaking hands with the Samaritan to seal the deal.

Can you begin to understand the anger that had built up for generations inside the Samaritan people, based on this level of rejection openly expressed toward them? The Jews felt superior to the Samaritans and had no problem openly showing their feelings. The Samaritans took every opportunity to strike out at the Jews, out of their anger and hatred.

There was a certain Samaritan woman, who was one of these rejected people. This woman had led such a hard life that she found herself even rejected by the other Samaritans. To divorce and remarry in Bible times was not the same as it is today. It was the worst disgrace any woman could experience, next to being barren. This woman felt so much rejection by her own town's people that she made her visit to the town well to draw water at high noon, not in the early morning or the cool of the evening as others did.

As Jesus approached Sychar, this Samaritan woman's home town, he told his disciples that he was getting a little weary and wanted to rest on Jacob's well. Some of the disciples volunteered to go into town and buy lunch for everyone, but at least John, and possibly some of the others, stayed at the well with Jesus. We know John was there, because he is the only one of the four Gospel authors who included this story in his account of the gospel of Jesus Christ.

After most of the disciples headed into town for food and Jesus had sat on Jacob's well for a few minutes, along came this Samaritan woman to the well to draw water. She hesitated for a moment, after seeing Jesus on the well, then proceeded to get her water. She did not expect any type of trouble from this Jew, since most Jews would simply ignore the Samaritans around them.

But as she began to pull up the first vessel of water, Jesus broke the silence by speaking to her.

"Give me a drink?" Jesus asked.

Startled by this Jew's boldness, the woman of Samaria: looked up quickly at Jesus, then raised her body slowly as she gazed at Jesus seriously.

"How is it that you, being a Jew, ask me—a woman of Samaria—for a drink?" she asked deliberately. Then her tone turned sarcastically bitter. "I thought Jews have nothing to do with Samaritans!"

Feeling confident that she had made it quite clear that she did not want to converse with this Jew, the Samaritan women returned to the strenuous job of pulling her pot out of the well.

"If you knew the gift of God," Jesus gently proceeded, "and who it is who asks you for a drink, you would have asked Him for a drink." Reaching down to the woman, Jesus finished lifting her pot out of the well for her, and said, "And He would have given you 'living water'."

Snatching the pot from Jesus' hands, the woman quickly responded, "Sir, you have nothing to draw water with, and the well is deep—from where, then, do you have this living water?" The woman glared defiantly at Jesus. "Are you greater than our father Jacob, who gave us this well and drank from it himself as did his children and his cattle?"

Feeling confident that she had finally shut Jesus up, the woman resumed her task of collecting her daily water.

Looking away, Jesus continued, "Whoever drinks of this water shall thirst again: But," Jesus turned lovingly toward her, "whoever drinks of the water that I shall give him shall never thirst; but the water that I shall give him shall be in him a well of water springing up into everlasting life."

Frustrated that she had not been able to get her message across to Jesus through anger that she did not want to engage in a conversation, the woman of Samaria stood and faced Jesus with her fists on her hips.

In the most sarcastic and mocking tones, she said, "Sir, give me this water so that I do not thirst or have to come here to draw water again."

"All right," Jesus responded. "But first, go call your husband and come back so I can give it to both of you."

Jesus' words struck her in the chest like a fist, and she gasped for her breath. Embarrassed, she turned away and looked down. "I have no husband," she responded.

"You have well said that you have no husband," Jesus continued. "For you have had five husbands in the past; and he whom you now have is not your husband." Jesus smiled, "so I guess in what you said you spoke truly."

Like a fighter in a ring hit by a one/two punch, the woman felt helpless to defend herself from such love and truth. Weakness overtook her, as her mind raced to come up with an appropriate reaction. Then she conceived a most brilliant plan for her counter attack.

"Sir," she began with a sense of confidence, "I perceive that you are a prophet, a Holy man." In her mind she was thinking, "and if you are anything like all the other religious people, all I have to do is ask you a deep, theological question, and you'll spend the next thirty minutes expounding your answer to me. That way you will forget all about me and my 'sin'." She proceeded with her plan, "Tell me, sir, there's something I've always wanted to ask a religious leader. Our fathers worshipped in this mountain; but you Jews say that in Jerusalem is the place where men should worship. I was wondering, sir," she tilted her head and fluttered her eyes, "which is correct?"

Jesus, with all sincerity and love, looked into her eyes, touching her hand, answered without hesitation. "My dear lady, believe me, the hour is coming when you shall neither worship the Father in this mountain, nor at Jerusalem. You see, you Samaritans worship a god that you do not know. We Jews at least know about the God we worship, for salvation is coming through the Jews. But the hour is coming, and now is when the true worshippers shall worship the Father in spirit and in truth. The Father is seeking this kind of worshipper to worship him. You see, God is a Spirit—and they who worship him must worship him in spirit and in truth."

"What did He just say?" the woman of Samaria thought to herself.

"And He's already finished! I've never heard anything like this before! Who is this guy?" Then she began to think out loud. "I know that the Messiah is supposed to be coming, who is called Christ, and that when He comes, He will be able to tell us everything."

Jesus responded gently, "I that speak unto you am He."

Realizing she was face to face with the Christ, the Son of God, the woman of Samaria began to weep and sank to her knees, grabbing Jesus' robe. "My Lord! My Lord!" she cried out.

Jesus reached down and raised her to her feet, looked straight into her eyes, and with a smile said, "My daughter, you are forgiven."

Discovering Acceptable Expressions of Worship

Now let's read Jesus' short teaching on worship from the scripture.

> *Jesus saith unto her, Woman, believe me, the hour cometh, when ye shall neither in this mountain, nor yet at Jerusalem, worship the Father. Ye worship ye know not what: we know what we worship: for salvation is of the Jews. But the hour cometh, and now is, when the true worshipers shall worship the Father in spirit and in truth: for the Father seeketh such to worship him. God is a Spirit: and they that worship him must worship him in spirit and in truth. John 4:21–24 KJV*

Here are a few important observations from this passage of scripture.

1. Jesus pointed out that a time was coming when worship would no longer be thought of as associated with a physical location, like Jerusalem or a mountain.
2. Jesus informed us that this worship, which was to come, would be "true" worship.
3. That meant the worship known at this point in history by both the Samaritans and the Jews was not true worship.
4. Before this time, all worship was symbolic worship, which foreshadowed the true worship to come.

5. "... the hour cometh, and now is..." because Jesus had arrived on the scene. The coming of Christ marked the beginning of "true worship."
6. True worship of God is "in spirit and in truth."

What Is True Worship?

I have introduced the topics of "in Christ" and "truth" in previous chapters. Please permit me to revisit and add to them here. Worship "in spirit and in truth" is the only "true" worship. Every expression of "true" worship must be initiated by the true Spirit of the Almighty God or else it is false worship. Likewise, the expressions of worship must line up with, or be validated by, the truth of God or it is also false worship.

What is Worship "In Spirit"

The short answer to this question is found in this scripture.

For as many as are led by the Spirit of God, these are sons of God. Romans 8:14 NKJV

To be in the Spirit is to be led by the Spirit of God who is inside us joined to our spirit. A Christian should be led by the Spirit every minute of every day. If we do that, we will continually do God's will for our lives, which includes worshipping God.

There is a problem accomplishing that, however, because our body and soul have not yet been redeemed. These two parts of our being are still controlled by the sin nature of mankind and are considered the enemy of the Spirit.

For to be carnally minded is death, but to be spiritually minded is life and peace. Because the carnal mind is enmity against God; for it is not subject to the law of God, nor indeed can be. So then, those who are in the flesh cannot please God. But you are not in the flesh but in the Spirit, if indeed the Spirit of God dwells in you. Romans 8:6–9 NKJV

The largest word in the English language has only two letters in it—"if." This simple little word is so huge because it always indicates a condition. For the first statement before the "if" to be true, the condition after the "if" must be met. In this case, the condition is that the Spirit of God must "dwell" in us. For the Spirit of God to "dwell" in us, it means He is there to be in charge of our life. Jesus abides where He is Lord. If that condition is met, then the result will be that we will be "in the Spirit." If Jesus has not set up His kingdom within us, He is just a guest and we are not "in the Spirit."

There is a difference between being "in the Spirit" and the Spirit being "in us." At the beginning of a relationship with the Lord, the Spirit of Christ comes to live on the inside of us.

> *What? know ye not that your body is the temple of the Holy Ghost which is in you, which ye have of [from] God, 1 Corinthians 6:19 KJV*

A person cannot consider himself or herself as a Christian unless he or she contains the Spirit of God in his or her being.

> *. . . Now if any man have not the Spirit of Christ, he is none of his. And if Christ be in you, the body is dead because of sin; but the Spirit is life because of righteousness. But if the Spirit of him that raised up Jesus from the dead dwell in you, he that raised up Christ from the dead shall also quicken your mortal bodies by his Spirit that dwelleth in you. Romans 8:9–11 KJV*

Christ's Spirit within us is the starting of a relationship with God. Us in Christ, or in the Spirit, is the goal of our relationship with God. And there is only one way to move from simply having Christ's Spirit inside us to us being in Christ, or in the Spirit.

> *But the anointing which ye have received of him abideth in you, and ye need not that any man teach you: but as the same anointing teacheth you of all things, and is truth, and is no lie, and even as it hath taught you, ye shall abide in him. 1 John 2:27 KJV*

To be in the "Spirit" or "in Christ" is to simply be taught and led by the Spirit of Christ, under His Lordship. To the degree that the Lord has taught, instructed, or led us is the degree that we "abide in Him." . . .and even as [to the degree that] it hath taught you, ye shall abide in him.[37]

The words "teach," "teacheth," and "taught" in this verse are different tenses of the same Greek word: *didasko* (did-as'-ko). The Strong's number is 1321. It can mean: "2a) to impart instruction (or direction) [to a humble follower or disciple]."[38]

To be "in the Spirit" is to allow the Spirit of God, who has joined Himself to our spirit, to teach, instruct, or lead us and for us to submit to that teaching humbly.

If we allow the Spirit of God to teach us, in the areas that we have been taught by Him, we are considered to be "in Christ" or in the Spirit of Christ or in the Spirit. The old ways of thinking and doing things, according to the flesh, have then disappeared; and everything about that aspect of our life has become new.

> *Therefore if any man be in Christ, he is a new creature: old things are passed away; behold, all things are become new. 2 Corinthians 5:17 KJV*

Let me reiterate this for you again. In the areas of life that we have allowed God to teach us by His Spirit through the Word of God, those areas are "in Christ" or under the Lordship of Jesus through His Spirit living inside us. In those areas, the old ways of thinking, feeling, and acting are passed away and in those areas *all* things have become new!

For us to move from the Spirit of Christ simply being "in us" to us being "in the Spirit," we must humbly submit ourselves to the teaching, leading, and Lordship of the Holy Spirit.

To worship the Lord "in Spirit" is to humbly follow His lead as to how we express our worship to God at any given moment!

---

[37] 1 John 2:27 (KJV).
[38] Strong, *Strong's Concordance.*

What is Worship "In Truth"

To discover what worship "in truth" is, let's first look at this concise study on "truth."

1. Truth came by Jesus Christ.

   For the law was given by Moses, but grace and truth came by Jesus Christ. John 1:17 KJV

2. Jesus is the truth.

   Jesus saith unto him, I am the way, the truth, and the life: no man cometh unto the Father, but by me. John 14:6 KJV

3. Jesus, the truth, first revealed Himself in the Old Testament scriptures called the "Law," which is the truth revealed as the written Word of God.

   Thy righteousness is an everlasting righteousness, and thy law is the truth. Psalms 119:142 KJV

4. All of God's Word is the truth, including the Old and New Testaments.

   They are not of the world, even as I am not of the world. Sanctify them through thy truth: thy word is truth. John 17:16–17 KJV

5. The written and spoken Word of truth from God is Spiritually alive.

   It is the spirit that quickeneth (makes alive); the flesh profiteth nothing: the words that I speak unto you, they are spirit, and they are life. John 6:63 KJV

6. Jesus Christ is the true revelation of God to mankind, the "Word" come in the flesh, living among us, the only revelation of Himself God has sent to mankind. God is revealed to us in both the living written/spoken Word and the living in-the-flesh Word. Both of these are the same revelation of God.

And the Word was made flesh, and dwelt among us, (and we beheld his glory, the glory as of the only begotten of the Father,) full of grace and truth. John 1:14 KJV

7. The Word teaches us, and directs our paths by enlightening us to the truth.

Thy word is a lamp unto my feet, and a light unto my path. Psalms 119:105 KJV
Through the tender mercy of our God; whereby the dayspring from on high hath visited us, To give light to them that sit in darkness and in the shadow of death, to guide our feet into the way of peace. Luke 1:78–79 KJV

8. In addition to the Word teaching and guiding us, God's abiding presence in our lives, the Spirit of God who anoints us, also teaches us all things spiritual. God's manifestation of Himself in Sprit is truth, just like God's manifestation in flesh or Word is truth, and together they are our teacher.

But the anointing which ye have received of him abideth in you, and ye need not that any man teach you: but as the same anointing teacheth you of all things, and is truth, and is no lie, and even as it hath taught you, ye shall abide in him. 1 John 2:27 KJV

9. The Word of God is truth.

Sanctify them through thy truth: thy word is truth. John 17:17 KJV

10. The Spirit of God is truth.

And I will pray the Father, and he shall give you another Comforter, that he may abide with you for ever; Even the Spirit of truth; whom the world cannot receive, because it seeth him not, neither knoweth him: but ye know him; for he dwelleth with you, and shall be in you. John 14:16–17 KJV

11. The Spirit of Truth, and the revealed Word of Truth, both teach us the same truth. They do not contradict each other, they are both manifestations of the same truth.

(Jesus said) I have yet many things to say unto you, but ye cannot bear them now. Howbeit when he, the Spirit of truth, is come, he will guide you into all truth: for he shall not speak of himself; but whatsoever he shall hear, that shall he speak: and he will show you things to come. He shall glorify me: for he shall receive of mine, and shall show it unto you. John 16:12–14 KJV

Conclusions From Our Study on Truth

The Spirit and the Word will always agree! What does this mean to us in regards to expressing worship to God? Simply this:

1. The Spirit of God is on the inside of us initiating worship continually.
2. Worship is the expression of our love for God.
3. The Spirit is initiating expressions of love from us in the same way a bridegroom initiates the expressions of love from his bride.
4. The expressions of our love for God, which the Spirit of God initiated inside us, will never degrade us as a human being. Love exalts—it does not debase.
5. The Spirit of Truth will never initiate an expression of worship that the written Word of Truth cannot validate!

Validating Physical Expressions of Worship

The physical expressions of worship that are acceptable to God are found in the Bible, the Word of Truth, in one of four ways: commandments, exhortations, examples, or prophesies.

A validation scripture in the form of a **commandment** is God requiring us through His Word to express our love to Him with our bodies in a particular way. Commandments are not optional. We have no right as children of God to choose not to respond to the Lord in ways indicated by commandments.

An **exhortation** scripture is God encouraging us through His Word to express our worship to Him in a particular way. When the Spirit solicits worship from us to be expressed in one of these ways, we gladly respond with that expression of love to Him, because He has already told us in scripture that this expression is how He wants to be worshipped.

An **example** scripture is God revealing to us, through His Word, ways that others in history have expressed their worship to God that have been acceptable to God. The examples show us that if those people expressed worship to God in a particular way and God received it from them as a valid expression of worship (and recorded it in His written Word for us to read), then when we sense His Spirit asking us to respond to Him with that expression of worship, we know God will receive it from us as well. Through examples in the Bible, we confirm the Holy Spirit's leading within us.

A **prophetic** scripture is God foretelling through one of His prophets an expression of worship that will be done in the future that will bring pleasure to God. From these scriptures, we know that when the Spirit of God initiates that expression of love to Jesus, He will receive it with joy.

Therefore, worshipping in Spirit and in Truth happens as the Word tells us how God wants us to physically express our love to Him, and the Spirit solicits when He wants our love expressed to Him in a particular way.

As an exercise to underline this point, let's look at an example of each of these types of validation scriptures using the biblical expression of worship: singing.

+ Commandment

Sing praises to God, sing praises: sing praises unto our King, sing praises. Psalms 47:6 KJV

+ Exhortation

And Miriam answered them, Sing ye to the LORD, for he hath triumphed gloriously; the horse and his rider hath he thrown into the sea. Ex 15:21 KJV

+ Example

I will be glad and rejoice in thee: I will sing praise to thy name, O thou most High. Psalms 9:2 KJV

+ Prophetic

And I will give her her vineyards from thence, and the valley of Achor for a door of hope: and she shall sing there, as in the days of her youth, and as in the day when she came up out of the land of Egypt. Hosea 2:15 KJV

Let's do the same exercise using bowing or bowing the knees as the expression of worship. Note: The first scripture here is both a commandment and a prophesy.

+ Commandment

For it is written, As I live, saith the Lord, every knee shall bow to me, and every tongue shall confess to God. Romans 14:11 KJV

+ Exhortation

O come, let us worship and bow down: let us kneel before the LORD our maker. Psalms 95:6 KJV

+ Example

*Wherewith shall I come before the LORD, and bow myself
before the high God? Micah 6:6 KJV*

+ Prophetic

*I have sworn by myself, the word is gone out of my mouth
in righteousness, and shall not return, That unto me every
knee shall bow, every tongue shall swear. Isaiah 45:23 KJV*

Biblical Expressions of Worship

In *Biblical Worship*, I wrote about the difference between the
synonyms of the word "worship" and the actual physical expressions of
worship. In that book, we researched the different synonyms of "worship."
In this chapter, let's examine the various biblical expression of worship
that we can do with different parts of our body. Remember, our body
must be used to express our love for God or man. "Worship" is what we
call the expression of love to God.

The expressions of worship found in the Bible can be divided into two
different categories: 1) expressions of worship that are posture positions
and 2) expressions of worship that are actions our body performs.

Let me list for you the different physical expressions of worship I have
discovered in the Bible so far. I do not claim that this is an exhaustive list.
I am sure there are more expressions of worship in the Bible than these.
I am listing these worship expressions systematically, according to the
parts of the body used for each expression.

It is true that some of these expressions affect more of the body
than just the parts doing the expression. These expressions are listed
under the body parts that performs the expression. For instance,
walking affects the entire body, yet we will list it under the feet and legs.

Type of scripture abbreviations: C = Commandment, En = Encouragement/
Exhortation, Ex = Example, P = Prophetic

Biblical Expressions of Worship

Type	Expression	Posture	Action
	Mouth		
1.	Sing		✓
Ex	*Now when they began to sing and to praise, the Lord set ambushes against the people of Ammon, Moab, and Mount Seir, who had come against Judah; and they were defeated. 2 Chronicles 20:22 NKJV*		
2.	Talk/speak/say		✓
Ex	*So He said, "No, but as Commander of the army of the Lord I have now come." And Joshua fell on his face to the earth and worshiped, and said to Him, "What does my Lord say to His servant?" Joshua 5:14 NKJV*		
3.	Shout		✓
En	*Oh come, let us sing to the Lord! Let us shout joyfully to the Rock of our salvation. Psalm 95:1 NKJV*		
4.	Pray		✓
C	*Continue earnestly in prayer, being vigilant in it with thanksgiving; Colossians 4:2 NKJV*		
5.	Eat		✓
P	*All the prosperous of the earth Shall eat and worship; Psalm 22:29 NKJV*		
6.	Laugh		✓
Ex	*Then our mouth was filled with laughter, And our tongue with singing. Then they said among the nations, "The Lord has done great things for them." Psalm 126:2 NKJV*		
7.	Cry (aloud)		✓
P, Ex	*The righteous cry out, and the Lord hears, And delivers them out of all their troubles. Psalm 34:17 NKJV*		
8.	Pant		✓
Ex	*I opened my mouth, and panted: for I longed for thy commandments. Psalms 119:131 KJV*		

9.	Declare		✓
En	*Let them give glory to the Lord, And declare His praise in the coastlands. Isaiah 42:12 NKJV*		
	Eyes		
10.	Lift		✓
Ex	*Unto You I lift up my eyes, O You who dwell in the heavens. Psalm 123:1 NKJV*		
11.	Weep/cry		✓
Ex	*Now while Ezra was praying, and while he was confessing, weeping, and bowing down before the house of God, a very large assembly of men, women, and children gathered to him from Israel; Ezra 10:1 NKJV*		
	Head and Face		
12.	Lift	✓	
P	*Now when these things begin to happen, look up and lift up your heads, because your redemption draws near." Luke 21:28 NKJV*		
13.	Bow	✓	
Ex	*Then the man bowed down his head and worshiped the Lord. Genesis 24:26 NKJV*		
	Hands and Arms		
14.	Lift or raise	✓	
Ex	*And Ezra blessed the Lord, the great God. Then all the people answered, "Amen, Amen!" while lifting up their hands. And they bowed their heads and worshiped the Lord with their faces to the ground. Nehemiah 8:6 NKJV*		
15.	Clap		✓
En	*Oh, clap your hands, all you peoples! Shout to God with the voice of triumph! Psalm 47:1 NKJV*		
16.	Play musical instruments		✓
Ex	*Then David and all Israel played music before God with all their might, with singing, on harps, on stringed instruments, on tambourines, on cymbals, and with trumpets. 1 Chronicles 13:8 NKJV*		

17.	Make physical art		✓
Ex	*He has filled them with skill to do all manner of work of the engraver and the designer and the tapestry maker, in blue, purple, and scarlet thread, and fine linen, and of the weaver—those who do every work and those who design artistic works. Exodus 35:35 NKJV*		
18.	Spread Out	✓	
Ex	*Then Solomon stood before the altar of the Lord in the presence of all the assembly of Israel, and spread out his hands 2 Chronicles 6:12 NKJV*		
19.	Wave		✓
Ex	*and he put all these in Aaron's hands and in his sons' hands, and waved them as a wave offering before the Lord. Leviticus 8:28 NKJV*		
20.	Use flags and banners		✓
Ex	*and we will shout for joy when you succeed [are victorious; as in battle], and we will raise a flag [banner] in the name of our God. May the Lord give you [fulfill] all that you ask for. Psalm 20:5 EXB*		
21.	Write		✓
Ex	*Then Eliakim the son of Hilkiah, who was over the household, Shebna the scribe, and Joah the son of Asaph, the recorder, came to Hezekiah with their clothes torn, and told him the words of the Rabshakeh. Isaiah 36:22 NKJV*		
	Legs and feet		
22.	Kneel/bow knees	✓	✓
Ex	*And so it was, when Solomon had finished praying all this prayer and supplication to the Lord, that he arose from before the altar of the Lord, from kneeling on his knees with his hands spread up to heaven. 1 Kings 8:54 NKJV*		
23.	Leap		✓
C	*Rejoice in that day and leap for joy! For indeed your reward is great in heaven, For in like manner their fathers did to the prophets. Luke 6:23 NKJV*		

24.	Walk (and leap)		✓
Ex	*So he, leaping up, stood and walked and entered the temple with them—walking, leaping, and praising God. Acts 3:8 NKJV*		
25.	Run		✓
Ex	*And when he was gone forth into the way, there came one running, and kneeled to him, and asked him, Good Master, what shall I do that I may inherit eternal life? Mark 10:17 KJV*		
26.	Dance		✓
En	*Let Israel rejoice in their Maker; Let the children of Zion be joyful in their King. Let them praise His name with the dance; Let them sing praises to Him with the timbrel and harp. Psalms 149:2–3 NKJV*		
27.	Stand	✓	
Ex	*Then the king stood by a pillar and made a covenant before the Lord, to follow the Lord and to keep His commandments and His testimonies and His statutes, with all his heart and all his soul, to perform the words of this covenant that were written in this book. 2 Kings 23:3 NKJV*		
	Entire Body		
28.	Bow	✓	✓
Ex	*And it came to pass, when Abraham's servant heard their words, that he worshiped the Lord, bowing himself to the earth. Genesis 24:52 NKJV*		
29.	Tremble		✓
En	*Oh, worship the Lord in the beauty of holiness! Tremble before Him, all the earth. Psalm 96:9 NKJV*		
30.	Sit	✓	
Ex	*Then all the children of Israel, and all the people, went up, and came unto the house of God, and wept, and sat there before the LORD, and fasted that day until even, and offered burnt offerings and peace offerings before the LORD. Judges 20:26 KJV*		
31.	Fall on face	✓	✓
P	*And thus the secrets of his heart are revealed; and so, falling down on his face, he will worship God and report that God is truly among you. 1 Corinthians 14:25 NKJV*		

32.	Fall down	✓	✓
P	*Yes, all kings shall fall down before Him; All nations shall serve Him. Psalm 72:11 NKJV*		
33.	Fast		✓
En	*Is it a fast that I have chosen, A day for a man to afflict his soul? Is it to bow down his head like a bulrush, And to spread out sackcloth and ashes? Would you call this a fast, And an acceptable day to the Lord? Isaiah 58:5 NKJV*		
34.	Production/processional/parade		✓
Ex	*David was clothed with a robe of fine linen, as were all the Levites who bore the ark, the singers, and Chenaniah the music master with the singers. David also wore a linen Ephod. Thus all Israel brought up the ark of the covenant of the Lord with shouting and with the sound of the horn, with trumpets and with cymbals, making music with stringed instruments and harps. And it happened, as the ark of the covenant of the Lord came to the City of David, that Michal, Saul's daughter, looked through a window and saw King David whirling and playing music; and she despised him in her heart. 1 Chronicles 15:27–29 NKJV*		

Table XIX

For something fun to do, get a concordance and see if you can find other scriptures validating these expressions of worship. You may also find other expressions that I have left out of this list.

Nonbiblical Expressions of Worship

Will the Spirit of God ever initiate expressions of worship from us that cannot be validated in the Bible? Remember, God's revelations confirm themselves, in that His Spirit and His Word always agree.

Therefore, I believe, it is impossible for the Spirit to initiate an expression of worship that the Word of God will not confirm. This point is vital for us to understand and follow, especially within our corporate worship gatherings!

Without this principle being established and followed, well-meaning Christians will continue to be deceived into expressing worship to God in ways that are not confirmed in the Word.

Back in the 1990s, a revival move of God took place in Toronto, Ontario, Canada. During that time, I personally experienced people barking like dogs, clucking like chickens, howling like wolves, and hissing like snakes in a time of worship. None of these expressions are validated in scripture; as such, we should not engage in expressing ourselves in worship in these ways!

In the 1980s, I heard one pastor, a dear friend, tell his congregation as he was introducing me to speak on worship that it did not matter what we did to express our worship to God as long as our heart was right. He went on to say that we could even do something as ridiculous as stand on our head and clap our feet together and God would receive it as worship.

I had to get up and teach on worship after that introduction, but I felt I could not let that statement ride. I simply responded by asking the pastor, in front of everyone, to find in the Bible where someone had stood on his or her head and clapped his or her feet together as an expression of worship. Of course, he couldn't do that, because it's not in the Bible. At the same time, I was aware of the inner conflict that pastor had struggled with over people dancing as an expression of worship. I can't understand why some people want to invent extra expressions of worship, when some of us haven't yet gotten comfortable with expressing ourselves in worship in all the ways the Bible reveals that we should express worship.

Another dear pastor friend told me once how the pianist of his church apparently got so overcome by the "Holy Spirit" in the middle of the worship service that she began clucking like a chicken with her hands in her arm pits flapping her elbows up and down. She left the piano bench, flapping and clucking all over the sanctuary. I was told that she stopped several times in front of different people, reached out and touched them, and they started clucking and flapping too. When this happened, all worship ceased and everyone was engrossed with the clucking and flapping of many people, who were deceived into thinking they were glorifying God. There was no attention being directed to Jesus at that time. Jesus wasn't getting any glory.

The pastor concluded his story to me by telling me that this turn of events went on so long that he wasn't able to preach that Sunday. "It was great!" he said.

"Are you telling me you didn't have a sermon prepared for that Sunday?" I asked.

Of course, he had prepared a sermon; and he told me that, prior to this clucking and flapping happening, he really felt he had a timely word from God for the congregation. My response to him was that he did have a word from God for the congregation and that he had been demonically deceived into not delivering that word.

"That can't be true," the pastor defended himself.

"Well," I answered, "if you can find any place in the scriptures where someone clucked like a chicken and flapped his or her arms like wings as an expression of worship, then I will change my judgment on the event."

Of course, he could not.

We cannot compromise on this point. Either the Bible is the revealed word of God or it is not. Either God has put all things pertaining to life and Godliness[39] in His word or He has not. Either God has told us in His word how he wants to be worshipped or He has left it entirely up to us to choose how we want to worship Him. However, if He has left it up to us to decide how we will worship Him, He will have to apologize to Cain for telling him his expression of worship was not acceptable.

We must worship in Spirit and in Truth! God's Word of Truth tells us all of the ways we can express our worship to God. Then the resident Holy Spirit within us leads us to express our love to God with one or more of these Biblical ways, when He prompts us to do them.

---

[39] 2 Pet. 1:3.

Chapter 7

Natural & Unnatural Expressions

God-Given Natural Expressions

It is my belief, although I cannot prove it by scripture, that God gives every one of us a way which we can express ourselves more easily than any other ways. I call this our natural expression. I have come to believe this by simply observing humanity over my lifetime.

For instance, I believe my mother's natural expression was tears or weeping. The reason I say that is because whenever she was sad, she cried; whenever she was happy, she cried; whenever she was any emotion, she cried. And there were lots of times we didn't know why she was crying, but she cried.

As a child, I appreciated her tears, especially when I was crying. But as a teenager, I grew to despise them. My mother's tears began to embarrass me, because she would cry in public.

My friends would ask me, "What's wrong with your mother?"

I'd have to answer them, "She just cries a lot; I don't know why."

The general consensus from all of the onlookers was that something must be desperately wrong with my mother, because of all the crying she did. So, every time my mother cried, I would ask her what was wrong.

Many times she responded with, "Nothing's wrong, honey, I'm just happy."

"You certainly have a strange way of showing it," I thought to myself.

This went on until, in my teenage wisdom, I felt it was my place to straighten my mother out about this crying thing. So, one day I sat her down in her room to address the issue.

"You just need to get a hold of your emotions and not cry so much," I concluded my remarks to her.

She had listened intently as I had expressed how embarrassed I was with all her crying, but now it was her turn to speak.

"I'm sorry my crying embarrasses you," she began, "but it's just not that easy for me to not cry."

I took a breath so I could cut in with something like, "But you have to try." However, I stopped short of making a sound when I saw the look in her eyes. This was painful for her too, so I waited for her to finish.

"I want to tell you a story," she began again, "of when I was about your age. All the time I was growing up, the kids would tease me about my crying. They called me 'cry baby' and other names. When I became a teenager, I was known as the girl who would cry at the drop of a hat. The older I got as a teen, the more I despised the way God had made me. I did not want to cry all the time as I was doing, so one day I asked God to take my tears away from me, and He did.

"The next year and a half was the worst time in my life. I had no way of expressing my feelings, and after a while, I became the most miserable person on the face of the earth. I ached for a way that I might express myself, but I found no way, because I had despised the way God made me to express myself. When I finally realized this, I lay across my bed one day in physical pain from the withheld emotions and begged God to give me back my tears. I promised Him that, if He gave me back my tears, I would never again despise that He had made me to express myself this way. I told Him I would never again be ashamed to cry."

"So, what happened?" I eagerly asked.

"I cried for three days straight," she responded.

"I'm sorry, Mother," I said and began to cry myself. "I will never again be ashamed of the way God made you. You cry as much as you want to."

After this experience, I wondered what way God had given to me to naturally express myself. I certainly wasn't a crier like my mother, but I kept wondering what way God gave me to express myself and what way God gave others to express themselves.

While trying to discover the answers to these questions, I began quietly observing people to see if their natural expressions were as obvious as my mother's. Believe it or not, when I started looking, I saw that there were some whose natural expressions were even more obvious than my mother's.

The first group of people I spotted were the talkers. These people always had to be talking, yet they didn't always make sense on a cognitive level. It was only when I realized they were expressing their feelings with their words, not information, that I began to understand them. Most of these people found it easy to pray, because it was easy for them to talk. Also, as they were faithful to worship God with their prayers, God developed them into the best intercessors I've ever known.

There were many other people who always, when expressing deep emotions, would automatically start using their hands to express themselves. I concluded by watching them that without their hands they would feel just as helpless at expressing themselves as my mother did without her tears. I even spoke to some of them and asked them to try to express themselves without using their arms, and they all found it impossible. These are the people who were the first to raise their hands in worship when God starting initiating that response from His church.

Then there are the people who are naturally loud. Even tender things that I would express slightly above a whisper, they would share loudly. I would notice that these are the people who found it very easy to shout in their worship expression. They also seemed to be the first of us to embrace the more demonstrative expressions of worship when God began initiating that sort of response from His people.

Then I observed people with very clear body language, not just the hands. These people are the ones who always had to be moving while worshipping, who also embraced dance as an expression of worship before anyone else did.

Some people I observed expressed themselves always with humility. These would be the first to close their eyes in worship or get into postures of humility and brokenness, even without being prompted. When it was time to pray, they would slip to their knees. When a song spoke of bowing or kneeling, they would many times assume that posture in their worship. It was this type of people who found it much easier to lie prostrate on the floor in a time of worship when God called for us all to express our love to Him in that way.

Even though I had observed all of these natural expressions in others, I was still struggling to know what my natural expression was. I finally broke down and asked God what it was. He quickly answered me, since He had been waiting all along for me to ask. "Music and, more specifically, writing and singing songs" was His answer to me. Then it began to all make sense. I thought of the many times and situations I had tried to express myself in spoken words, only to fail miserably. Then I remembered the times I was able to sing as an expression of my feelings, and I remembered the positive results and responses singing brought from other people. I could say anything I needed to say by singing it and everyone understood me. It was when I opened my mouth to talk that I was plagued with multiple levels of misunderstandings.

Families of Worship Expressions

Whatever our natural expression is, it is going to be the most comfortable for us to do. Unnatural expressions are not comfortable for us. They are uncomfortable for us to do and can be uncomfortable for us to be around when others are expressing themselves in those ways.

The physical expressions that are comfortable or uncomfortable to us are relevant to who we have become up to this present moment in our lives. Who we are is based on our personality. For example, a person who has a quiet personality would usually find shouting in worship very uncomfortable. In the same way, an individual with a demonstrative personality who is totally comfortable with worship expressions like shouting, or leaping might be uncomfortable in silence or "being still"[40] before the Lord.

There are five different families, or categories, of physical biblical

---

[40] Ps. 46:10.

expressions of worship. They are the Spoken-Word, Hand-Gesture, Demonstrative, Humble, and the Artistic Expressions. Every biblical physical expression of worship will fit into one of these categories or families of expressions. Here is the list of worship expressions from our last chapter divided alphabetically into their appropriate families.

Categories of Worshipers

A. Spoken-Word Expressions
   1. Declare
   2. Pray
   3. Speak
B. Hand-Gesture Expressions
   1. Clap
   2. Lift or Raise
   3. Spread Out
   4. Wave
C. Demonstrative Expressions
   1. Cry (aloud)
   2. Eat
   3. Exuberant dance
   4. Laugh
   5. Leap
   6. Pant
   7. Run
   8. Shout
   9. Stand
D. Humble Expressions
   1. Bow
   2. Bow Head
   3. Fast
   4. Kneel
   5. Lift Eyes
   6. Lift Up Head
   7. Prostration

        a. Fall Down
        b. Fall on Face
    8. Sit
    9. Tremble
    10. Walk
    11. Weep
  E. Artistic Expressions
    1. Expressive dance
    2. Flags and Banners
    3. Physical Art
    4. Play Music Instruments
    5. Production/Processional/Parade
    6. Sing
    7. Write

Each physical expression within a family of expressions is similar to the other expressions within that family. Therefore, progressing from our natural expression of worship to another expression in the same family is more comfortable to us.

For instance, the person who finds it within his or her personality to bow his or her head while worshipping will easily progress to the place where he or she will bow his or her body or knees while expressing worship to God. It would not be as easy for this person to leap and dance to express worship, because those expressions usually are uncomfortable to this personality type.

However, as we generalize in these examples for the sake of making the point, in reality it can be difficult to totally predict who might be comfortable expressing worship to God in certain ways. This is because each personality is unique and develops differently and at its own pace. Also, each personality is changing daily from all the different influences around it.

The Importance of Our Natural Expression

It has been my observation that every person needs to discover his or her one truly God-given way to express him- or herself first before progressing to other expressions, even the ones in the same family of expressions. If this does not happen first, it seems to be more difficult for us to truly express the depths of our being through other expressions. Any other worship expression we use, other than our natural expression, can easily become a performance of our personality, rather than an expression or an extension of ourselves. Conversely, when you first express your deep feelings with your natural expression, adding other expressions to that one will feel more natural or comfortable to us. It feels more like we are growing or maturing in our personality that way.

Some of us have long ago discovered our natural physical expression, some as early as elementary school. Others still struggle with this into adulthood. Of course, it doesn't help when no one has told us how important it is to discover our natural expression for our natural and spiritual growth.

If we have never discovered our one God-given expression of worship and way to express our emotions, then expressing worship to God can seem difficult. People who have not yet discovered their natural expression will conclude that there must be something wrong with them, since they are unable to express their love to God on a deep level like others do.

Cultural and Traditional Expressions of Worship

Perhaps the single most-effective reason people have never discovered their natural expression of worship is the culture or traditions they have grown up in. Culture refers mainly to nationalities or very large people groups. Even within these large people groups there can develop what are known as subcultures.

For many years, my wife Chris has had a ministry to the deaf and a ministry in training others to minister to the deaf. It is interesting to me, having lived both in the United States and Canada for extended periods of time, how both of these national societies have a deaf subculture that have many similarities yet are distinct because of the countries' cultural influences.

Traditions can refer to any size of people group, but most often it involves smaller people groups than even subcultures. In other words, the deaf subculture in Quebec, Canada, has a completely different set of traditions than the deaf subculture in British Columbia, Canada. And the deaf in northern British Columbia have different traditions than the deaf in Southern British Columbia. As a matter of fact, in the town of Prince George, British Columbia, where we lived for six years, different groups of deaf had developed their own traditions based on their geographical locations around the city and all sorts of other influences.

Our own families have their own traditions. In my family, our four children developed the tradition of watching *The Muppet Christmas Carol* every Christmas eve before retiring for the evening. Chris and I liked this tradition the kids developed, since it allowed us to sneak off to another part of the house to wrap their presents. Before this tradition, we had to wait till they went to sleep to wrap their presents.

So, what qualifies something to be a tradition? To most of us, anything we have done twice becomes a tradition. We go to church and sit in the same seat every Sunday, because it is our tradition. However, not doing something can also become a habit or a tradition as well. Pastor Mike Rosenau, whom I had the privilege of serving with in ministry in Prince George, British Columbia, told me a story about traditions that I found amusing.

A husband noticed, only after several years of marriage, that every time their family would have bratwurst for supper, his wife would cut the ends off before preparing them in her skillet. Finally, his curiosity got the best of him, and he asked his wife about this strange tradition she seemed to have. She had never really thought about it before—it was just something she always did.

"But why do you do it?" the husband persisted. "You have to have a reason for doing something like that.

"I don't know," the wife responded. Then remembering her childhood, she remarked, "I guess it is because my mother always cut the ends off of her bratwurst. I just assumed she had a good reason for it, so I've always done it that way."

"But what is the reason," the husband insisted, growing more and more frustrated.

Her husband's frustration prompted her to phone her mother, in the middle of the day at work, to ask her mother where this tradition started.

"I don't know," her mother answered. "Is it important?"

"Well, my husband seems to think it is," she responded, "and now my curiosity is driving me crazy."

The mother thought out loud. "All my sisters prepare bratwurst the exact same way. I wonder if there is a concentration of something bad in the ends."

"Mother," the daughter responded, getting more and more frustrated herself. "That's ridiculous."

"Well, I really don't know," mother pleaded for mercy. "I guess we girls all grew up watching your grandmother fix it that way, so we just assumed there was a good reason for it."

The phone call to the grandmother was almost identical to the one with her mother, and everyone's frustration levels grew. But two weeks later, the grandmother remembered. When she first started cooking for her husband, the only frying pan they had was a small one. That's when she discovered that she could get the bratwurst to lay in the skillet flat if she cut a half inch off of each end.

Of course, not knowing the reason for something is the danger of traditions, especially worship traditions. Jesus cautioned us about religious traditions.

> *And he said unto them, Full well ye reject the commandment of God, that ye may keep your own tradition. Mark 7:9 KJV*

Every Christian denomination and every church in that denomination has its own worship traditions. The churches adopt their denomination's traditions and add to those traditions many more of their own. There is nothing wrong with having a rich heritage of meaningful traditions. However, if your church can't answer the questions about its traditions, perhaps it is time to drop some of these meaningless traditions and create meaningful ones. However, I would investigate any traditions before you discontinue them. You may find there is a very important reason for the tradition, or you may find out that the tradition sprang out of something stupid like an undersized skillet.

Another reason to change your church's worship traditions is spiritual growth. Whereas a worship tradition established back in the 1940s may have reflected the level of spiritual revelation and growth of your church back then, do not sentence your church to spiritual stagnation by only conducting worship the way it was done at that time. Allow the old traditions that reflect yesterday's revelations to be replaced with new traditions that reflect today's revelations.

Worship Taboos

Culture and tradition will dictate the acceptable expressions of worship in your worship setting, as well as those expressions that are taboo.

To graduate from a university with a degree in church music, I was required to take a course called "The Organ and Its Literature." For that class, students had to write six full-length research papers about the development of the organ throughout church history. In doing the research for those papers, I learned that at one point in history churches traditionally considered the organ to be the devil's instrument. The author of a book I was reading cited his hunch that this tradition occurred because the Christians could still remember their fellow Christians being put to death in the great Coliseums of Europe to the sound of pipe organs. Interestingly enough, the churches that banned organs at that time reportedly worshipped to the sound of three staple musical instruments: the trumpet, the Jew's harp, and the drums.[41] By the late 19th century, most churches had embraced the organ as the staple musical instrument to accompany worship and had banned drums, making them the new instrument of the devil. This, of course, was perpetuated in the 20th century because of the wide-spread use of the drums in jazz, blues, and rock and roll music. The drums held that title till the 1970s, when contemporary Christian music was born.

---

[41] This paper has been lost.

If a person's natural expression is accepted within his or her culture and church worship traditions, it will be easy for that person to discover his or her natural expression of worship, because it will be encouraged. However, if a person's natural expression is taboo in the culture and/or church worship traditions, it will be next to impossible for the individual to discover it.

I was teaching on worship at a camp near Kansas City, Kansas, so I presented some of the material that is in this book. When I reached the place in the teaching where I wanted to list the different biblical expressions of worship, as in Chapter Six, I wrote them on a chalkboard. In those days, I had no printed notes to hand out, and those attending the seminars would have to write out all their own notes. I listed the different parts of the body—the eyes, the mouth, the head, the arms and hands, the legs and feet, and the entire body—and asked those attending the seminar to tell me ways that they were aware of that the Bible tells us we can express our worship to the Lord with these different body parts. As people spoke out different expressions of worship, I would quickly write them on the board under the appropriate body parts.

We were doing great, and collectively our class was coming up with almost every expression of biblical worship I have found in the Bible. When we reached the section on the legs and feet, people started shouting out things like leap, walk, run, etc. Then someone said the "D" word, and what happened next makes me cry to this day.

There was an older gentleman in our class who walked with a severe limp and required the use of a cane just to get around. Someone had shouted out the worship expression of dancing, which I had written on the board. Then the next expression someone called out was kneeling. I was in the middle of writing that word on the board when this old gentleman said, "Whoa, whoa, wait a minute. You have to go back to the one before. That can't be right! Dancing is not an expression of worship!"

"Why do you say that?" I asked.

"Because it isn't!" the man insisted. "I've known that all my life."

"Well, what do you base that on?" I asked him.

"It's what I've always been taught," the man insisted.

"By whom?" I continued to query him.

"By my church," his response came quickly.

"Do you mind," I asked him, "if I ask you what church you go to?"

"Of course not—I go to the Baptist church."

Now, I had grown up in a Baptist church. My father was a Baptist preacher. So, I was quite familiar with the fundamental Baptist's beliefs on dancing back in the late 1970s. My mother and father had explained it to me several times as I was growing up—that John the Baptist (our church's founder, they claimed) had been beheaded because of a dance. Therefore, all dancing was of the devil. I remember in elementary school when my gym class was doing a section on different types of dancing, my parents sent me to school with a note saying I could not participate in that class because of religious beliefs. For that, I was teased mercilessly by my classmates. Along with the note to my teacher, my parents had equipped me with several copies of a tract entitled "Ten Reasons Why I Do Not Dance." They told me if anyone wanted to know why I wasn't dancing, I was to give them one of those tracts.

It wasn't until years later, when I started reading the Bible on my own, that I realized dancing as an expression of worship was not only permitted by God but also commanded. Equipped with my personal Bible study on this subject, I began to share with this older man what I had found out about the dance as an expression of worship. The first scripture I turned to was this one.

> *Let Israel rejoice in him that made him: let the children of Zion be joyful in their King. Let them praise his name in the dance: let them sing praises unto him with the timbrel and harp. Psalms 149:2–3 KJV*

I pointed out that if it is wrong to dance, it is also wrong to sing, according to this scripture. If we are going to throw out part of a scripture, we have to throw out the whole thing. But since we are not permitted to add to or take away from the scriptures,[42] we have to accept the dance as a legitimate, biblical expression of worship just like we do singing. I then read him this confirmation scripture in the form of a commandment.

---

[42] Rev. 22:18–19.

> *Praise him with the timbrel and dance: praise him with*
> *stringed instruments and organs. Psalms 150:4 KJV*

Next, I talked to him about the time when King David and the children of Israel brought the Ark of the Covenant back to Jerusalem as an example confirmation scripture.

> *And as the ark of the LORD came into the city of David,*
> *Michal Saul's daughter looked through a window, and saw*
> *king David leaping and dancing before the LORD; and*
> *she despised him in her heart. 2 Samuel 6:16 KJV*

Here's a quick side thought. Just like Michal was not worshipping God or participating in the worship celebration, I find it is usually people who do not worship that are critical of other people's expressions of worship. If you are truly worshipping, you will not notice what is happening with other people around you.

"So, you see," I said to the older man, "dancing is OK as an expression of worship to God."

This dear old man began to weep in front of me and the class. He fought back the tears for several minutes and eventually gained his composure enough to talk.

"In my late teens and early twenties, I loved to dance," he told us. "I could express myself by dancing better than through any other way. I used to sneak into the night spots before I was old enough, because it was the only place I knew of that I could dance. Even after I was old enough to go to these places, I didn't go there to drink or smoke or for any of the other reasons people go to bars—I only went there to dance, because I was not aware of any other setting where dancing was permitted.

"Then," the older man went on, "someone told me about Jesus and how He died for my sins. When I heard the gospel for the first time, I knew I wanted to be 'saved.' So, I started to pray a 'sinner's prayer' to receive Jesus into my life when they stopped me and told me there was one more thing I needed to know. If I were to be saved, I would have to give up dancing, because it was of the devil.

"Faced with the choice of having my sins forgiven, having the King of the universe come live on the inside of me, and spending eternity in heaven or being able to dance, of course, I chose the Lord. However, it was the hardest thing I have ever done—to give up dancing.

"For my entire life since then, I have felt I had no way to express myself, and I've been totally frustrated because of this. I suppose if I had never discovered that I could express myself in the dance so completely, I wouldn't have been so frustrated. But I did, and I was." He began to clench his teeth. "And now you are telling me I could have been dancing all my life and that God would not be angry with me but would receive it with joy as worship to Him." Standing now, and trembling and leaning on his cane, he raised his voice through the pain in his soul and screamed, "I wish you had never told me this!" He began to cross the room to the door, struggling more with his limp now because of his acute emotions. "I wish I could have died having never known this, because now I'm a crippled old man. I can't dance now if I tried!" Stopping at the door, he turned back to me and yelled, "Why did you have to tell me this?" With that, he turned and left.

Needless to say, the class never recovered from that experience that night, and I found myself on my face before God for several weeks, seeking Him for wisdom about that experience. This is when God taught me about the effects of culture and tradition on finding our natural expression. And this lesson is etched into my being by the memory of the pain in that older man's face. May we never be found as church leaders to teach as doctrines the traditions of men!

> *He answered and said unto them, Well hath Esaias prophesied of you hypocrites, as it is written, This people honoureth me with their lips, but their heart is far from me. Howbeit in vain do they worship me, teaching for doctrines the commandments of men. Mark 7:6–7 KJV*

May we only teach the Word of God!

Responses to Unnatural Expressions of Worship

I have observed over the years a progression of responses and reactions in people when they are exposed to unnatural or taboo expressions of worship. Almost always, when someone is first exposed to a way of expressing worship that he or she has never witnessed or heard of before or an expression that is out of the family of expressions that the individual is most comfortable with, his or her first reaction is judgment. The judgment will be both against the expression and many times against the person doing it. Statements like "That can't be right!" or "That is not of God!" are inevitably used. Of course, there is just a short cognitive distance between something not being of God and it being of the devil. When we judge something as not being of God, what most of us mean is that it is of the devil.

Another popular phrase used to describe an expression of worship that someone is uncomfortable with is "They are worshipping *in* the flesh!" Such a statement is unbiblical in the context of worship. It is a perversion of the biblical phrase "in the Sprit." And since people have developed a natural and incorrect understanding of what "in the Spirit" means, they transfer this interpretation to the adaptation of the phrase "in the flesh." Based on this, they think it is correct to use the phrase "in the flesh" to represent the opposite of their interpretation of "in the Spirit." To understand the biblical phrase "in the Spirit," see Chapter Six.

The fact is, *every* expression of worship *must* be done by the flesh or body. It is not worship unless our flesh *is* involved. God gave us our bodies to us as the expresser of our being, so every expression of worship *must* be "in the flesh" or it is not biblical worship.

After people are exposed to an uncomfortable expression of worship for a while, they may develop a level of tolerance, especially if the people expressing worship to God in a way that is questionable are known to those who are judging. Tolerance is slower to develop when you do not know the people you are judging. However, if you know them, you will be forced to admit sooner or later that these people do not exhibit the type of spiritual fruit in their lives as those who are following the devil or their own flesh.

In other words, the longer you are exposed to an uncomfortable expression of worship, the more it becomes difficult for you to reconcile what you witness in the lives of the worshipers with your doctrine or traditions of worship. At some point, you will have to admit that something doesn't add up in what you have always believed. This will cause you to stop judging the other people and to begin to tolerate their expressions of worship.

Eventually you will accept both the people and their expression of worship that made you uncomfortable at first, as long as they don't expect you to express your worship that way. In other words, your attitude becomes, "It's all right for others to worship in that way, but I have my own way of expressing worship."

If you are ever required or think you are required by God or man to express worship to God in an uncomfortable way, no matter where you are in the judgment-tolerance-acceptance cycle, strong rebellion can surface. This attitude of rebellion is usually wrongly justified by our sense of self-preservation or our survival instinct. Statements like "That's just not me" are usually said to justify our self-preservation attitude.

Self-Preservation and Worship

Every one of us has a strong survival instinct that God has given us—and this is very good. Without it, many of us would not be alive today. The will to live is what keeps us from doing something stupid when we are in danger. Our self-preservation instincts cause us to drive properly, watch our step on a cliff, fight infections in our body, and the list goes on and on.

When confronted by danger, fear takes over every function of our mind so that we cannot think about anything other than what is causing us fear. God designed and programmed us that way for our self-preservation. Science calls this the "fight or flight" response.

While living in Canada, we drove through the Jasper and Banff national parks dozens of times. One of our favorite Canadian cities is

Banff, nestled in the Canadian Rockies. Year round, you will see elk and other wildlife feeding on the grass and vegetation throughout the city, many times in people's front yards or backyards. They are protected by law within the national parks.

Most of the time, the elk are extremely docile and coexist with humans with no problems. However, every year for a month or so, authorities post signs everywhere warning tourist to stay away from the elk, because it is rutting or mating season. The male elk are anything but docile during this time of year and will kill any creature that gets between them and their female.

It was that time of year and we had just arrived at the Banff Sulfur Hot Springs, parked the car, and were getting out of the car when we noticed a gigantic bull elk feeding on the grass strip down the center of the parking lot. The next thing I noticed was a guy with a camera and two young boys. The guy was telling his boys to go stand by the elk so he could take their picture. I'm guessing the boys to be about three and five years old. The kids were very nervous about being near the animal with the huge set of antlers, so they stopped about eight feet away.

"No, no," dad shouted. "Get right up close to him," he insisted.

The boys, with fear in their eyes, inched backward a couple of steps, displaying more common sense than their dad.

"No, that's not close enough," dad shouted. "Get closer!"

Not wanting to disappoint their dad, they walked back about three feet, about two-and-a-half feet from the bull elk.

I was just taking a breath to shout to the dad across the parking lot that the boys were too close for their safety when the elk raised his head from grazing. He then lowered his head to a fighting position and began to charge the boys. I was too far away to do anything.

When the dad saw his boys were going to be attacked, he screamed as loud as he could and ran toward the elk. The scream startled the elk, causing it to halt its attack long enough for the dad to grab his two boys and get them into their vehicle. Moments later, the elk resumed his attack, this time against the truck they were in.

I dare say that the fight-or-flight survival mode, which shuts out every other thought or emotion except the fear and what we are fearful of, saved those boys and that man's life that day. While trying to run for your life is not the time to think about where to get gas next. Too many open programs will slow your computer down, and any other thoughts at a time like this could slow your reaction time down enough to make a fatal difference.

Survival is a good thing, when it comes to our physical body, but that's the only part of our being that God intended for the survival instinct to function as protection. We get into trouble when we operate our survival instinct to preserve our soul or personality. God never intended for a Christian to use the survival instinct to preserve the soul. On the contrary, many scriptures instruct us completely opposite of this.

I protest (swear) by your rejoicing which I have in Christ
Jesus our Lord, I die daily. 1 Corinthians 15:31 KJV

In this scripture, Paul, the apostle who wrote the majority of the New Testament, tells us he dies daily. What part of his being is dying on a daily basis? It can't be his body, because it seems to be very strong at this time. Besides, do you actually believe that Paul's physical body died every day and then got miraculously resurrected again every morning, only to die again on the next day? No, this is not some spiritual *Groundhog Day* movie experience we're talking about.

Also, it cannot be Paul's spirit that died daily. By this time in Paul's life the Spirit of God had been joined to Paul's spirit for quite a few years. Since it is impossible for God's Spirit to ever die, it is also impossible for Paul's spirit to die.

That only leaves one part of Paul that could fit the description of dying daily: the soul. After all, it is in the mind and soul where we are undergoing the process of being saved or being delivered while on this earth. This means that the areas in our soul that are not subject to the Christ's lordship must die so that all things may become new in our lives. And this happens to the degree that we have been taught by God's Holy Spirit.

Our soul, the seat of our personality, must be subject to change every day. To act in self-preservation toward our soul and personality says we will no longer allow the Spirit and the Word of God to change us to be like Christ; and that is a very dangerous attitude to adopt! God's process of conforming us into His image includes the death of our current personality so that His personality for us can come alive. Our soul must be changed, yet it is impossible for the new man to come alive in us, unless the old man dies first.

> *But some man will say, How are the dead raised up? and with what body do they come? Thou fool, that which thou sowest is not quickened (made alive), except it die: 1 Corinthians 15:35–36 KJV*

For the soul to be made alive in Christ, it must first die, just like a natural seed when it is put into the ground. New life can only come after that seed's death. Likewise, our soul cannot be made alive in Christ until the old man dies first.

> *And Jesus answered them, saying, The hour is come, that the Son of man should be glorified. Verily, verily, I say unto you, Except a corn of wheat fall into the ground and die, it abideth alone: but if it die, it bringeth forth much fruit. John 12:23–24 KJV*

For years I thought this scripture was talking about Jesus dying on the cross and that through His death, burial, and resurrection there would be much fruit in the form of souls that He would bring into His kingdom. I thought this scripture was telling me that the way Jesus was to be glorified was through the cross and the "fruit" of souls who would be saved.

However, one day I read the verse in the context of the verses after it and was stunned to find out that this verse is not talking about Jesus' death at all. It is talking about *our* deaths being the context in which the Son of Man will be glorified. Here are the verses that immediately follow:

> *He that loveth his life shall lose it; and he that hateth his life in this world shall keep it unto life eternal. If any man*

serve me, let him follow me; and where I am, there shall also my servant be: if any man serve me, him will my Father honor. John 12:25–26 KJV

Jesus is not the one who loves His own life. He came to earth to lay down His life for us. These instructions are not directed toward Jesus—they are directed to us, God's people. They explain exactly how the Son of Man will be glorified, and they prove that we are the seed He was talking about that must die for the Lord to be glorified. Please read this scripture one more time with this in mind.

And Jesus answered them, saying, The hour is come, that the Son of man should be glorified. Verily, verily, I say unto you, Except a corn of wheat fall into the ground and die, it abideth alone: but if it die, it bringeth forth much fruit. John 12:23–24 KJV

The fruit here is the character of Christ, the fruit of the Spirit, or the image of Christ being formed in us.

The Image of Christ

Remember the declaration of God before He made man in the Genesis account of creation?

And God said, Let us make man in our image, after our likeness:. . . Genesis 1:26 KJV

God created mankind in both the image of God and in the likeness of God. The likeness of God refers to God's form. Our physical form is made according to God's form, which was discussed in Chapter Two.

The image of God is the personality, the morals, the character, and holiness of God. This is what was lost after Adam and Eve sinned, when they lost their place in the Garden of Eden. Therefore, the image of God is what has to be restored, according to Romans 8:29.

For whom he did foreknow, he also did predestinate to be conformed to the image of his Son, that he might be the firstborn among many brethren. Romans 8:29 KJV

What is the image or character of God that we need to be conformed to? Paul answers that for us. He tells us that the fruit or evidence that God's Spirit is present and working His character into our lives are these traits.

But the fruit of the Spirit is love, joy, peace, longsuffering, gentleness, goodness, faith, Meekness, temperance: against such there is no law. Galatians 5:22–23 KJV

Because we lost the image of God through Adam's sin, our personalities have been formed by the influences of a sinful world and our unregenerated flesh. Now our personalities need to be reformed after the image of God's personality.

Of course, every one of us are in a different stage of development in the process of becoming like Christ. The more like Christ we become, the easier it is for us to respond to the Spirit's initiation for us to express worship to Jesus in any biblical way—no matter if it is comfortable or uncomfortable to us.

When you look at Jesus' personality, it is impossible to fit Him into a particular personality category. At times, you see Jesus very recluse, and at other times you see Him being very demonstrative. Jesus' personality is outside the box that most psychologists would want Him to fit into.

When we become more like Jesus, we are able to express ourselves in worship in any way He desires from us. It's like the old spiritual. . . "I will pray when the Spirit says pray. I will sing when the Spirit says sing. I will shout when the Spirit says shout. I will dance when the Spirit says dance." . . . and on and on the verses could go, each verse ending with the phrase, "and obey the Spirit of the Lord."

The comfortable expressions of worship are the ones that fit into our personality, and the uncomfortable expressions are the ones that go against our personality. However, a Christian's personality should be in the process of being changed into the image of Christ by the influences of the washing of the water of God's Word[43] and God's presence that inhabits us[44] and our praise.[45]

Which Comes First, Comfort or Commandment?

Will God's Spirit ever initiate an expression of worship from us that is uncomfortable to us?

On the one hand, we know that God is a gentleman and will never force us to do something we are uncomfortable doing. On the other hand, we have God trying to kill our old nature so we can get to the place where we can express our love to Him in all of the biblical expressions of worship. So, what is the answer to our question?

The answer is yes. Yes, God will initiate expressions of worship from us that we are uncomfortable doing; but, just as He responded to Cain's self-willed worship, God will not respond to us in anger because we did not obey Him. God will simply continue prompting us to express our love to Him in these uncomfortable ways until we obey.

Trouble happens when we continue to say no to the Spirit's prompting. Disobedience is sin, and sin separates us from God's presence. Without being in God's presence, we are cut off from our very spiritual life source. When we receive no life through God's presence, the truth we receive becomes distorted and out of balance, because the Spirit is no longer able to be our teacher. We become deceived into thinking it is not necessary to spend time in God's presence to be a Christian. Then we teach our converts this deadly deception as well. Eventually, we blame God for our lack of intimacy in our relationship with Him and forget that the entire deception began with our disobedience to the Spirit's initiation of worship, because what He was asking was uncomfortable to our not-yet-redeemed soul and personality.

---

[43] Eph. 5:26.
[44] 1 Cor. 6:19.
[45] Ps. 22:3.

Progressive Worship Sacrifices

Throughout the Bible, worship has always been associated with sacrifice, and sacrifice has always meant something must die. In the Old Testament, the sacrifices were animals who shed their blood as a symbol of the Lamb of God to come, whose blood takes away the sin of the world. Jesus is the Lamb of God, the supreme and only sacrifice now needed to pay for the sins of the whole world.

> *The next day John seeth Jesus coming unto him, and saith,*
> *Behold the Lamb of God, which taketh away the sin of the*
> *world. John 1:29 KJV*

The "lamb" refers to the once-a-year sacrifice of a perfect, spotless lamb made by the high priest behind the heavy vale of the holiest of holies in the tabernacle. A lamb had to die every year for the sins of God's people, because the best the lamb's blood could do was symbolically "cover" the sins for a year. However, when Jesus came and shed His blood, it "took away" the sins of the world. Since Jesus, the perfect "Lamb" was sacrificed, His blood has taken away all the sins that had only been covered by the blood sacrifices in the past and all the sins which would be committed after His supreme sacrifice.

Our worship of God does not involve blood sacrifices, since Jesus paid the ultimate sacrifice as God's perfect lamb. However, just because we are not required to offer blood sacrifices in our worship of God today does not mean we do not still worship God out of sacrifice. The New Testament sacrifices involve death to the Christian's flesh, which is made up of our soul and our body.

Self-preservation will not allow our body to express itself in ways that are uncomfortable to our unregenerated soul. Therefore, the two New Testament sacrifices equated with worship found in scripture requires our body to express our heart to God as His Spirit leads, no matter what our soul thinks or wants.

By him therefore let us offer the sacrifice of praise to God
continually, that is, the fruit of our lips giving thanks to
his name. Hebrews 13:15 KJV

As we have pointed out several times, the starting place of our relationship with God happens when we realize we are a sinner and we need a Savior. But to enter into a Savior/sinner relationship with God requires that we make Jesus Lord of our lives. This only happens when we confess that Jesus is our Lord with our lips, as we believe in Him in our heart.[46] Of course, no one can declare Jesus is Lord except "by Him."[47] God's Spirit comes to us at the moment we are ready to confess Jesus is Lord and gives us the grace to do it. As soon as we experience the Spirit of God joined to our spirit on the inside of us, He begins to initiate worship from us to Jesus, and we automatically follow the confession of our lips that Jesus is Lord with giving Him thanks for being Lord.

But God does not want us to stop with only expressing our love to Him with our lips. He wants us to progress to the place where we can express our love to Him with our entire body. To get there will require several levels of sacrifice or dying to ourselves.

Therefore, I urge you, brothers, in view of God's mercy, to
offer your bodies as living sacrifices, holy and pleasing to
God—this is your spiritual act of worship. Romans 12:1NIV

So then, the New Testament sacrifices that God requires of us in the context of our worship of God are progressive. We start with expressing praise and thanksgiving with our lips and eventually get to the place where we can express our love to God with every part of our body.

This is also how God intended for all intimate relationships to develop. Since He tells us that the marriage relationship between a man and a woman is the picture of the type of relationship He desires to have with us, we can use the progression of that relationship to understand the expression of our love relationship with Jesus. When two people are

---

[46] Rom. 10:9–10.
[47] 1 Cor. 12:3.

just friends, the most physical expression of love in that relationship will be with words. As a couple is developing toward a deeper relationship, their growing love may be expressed with a slight touch of the hand and may progress to holding hands. These expressions may or may not reflect intimacy to some people and leave the other person wondering. However, there is no question of either person's desire for an intimate relationship once they share a kiss, the fruit of their lips. From that point, we need to follow God's plan for human intimacy. Only after a man and woman have, before God, entered into a binding, covenant relationship with each other are they to express their love for each other with progressively more of their body, until they are able to express their love to each other with their whole body.

Jesus is our betrothed. One day He will return to earth to redeem us as His bride. But until that day, we still can express our love to Him with our bodies in the ways He has told us about in the scriptures, by responding to His lead. Although many times I felt I was not ready to express my worship to the Lord in an additional way, when I have obeyed the Spirit's prompting, it was well worth the sacrifice it cost to be in God's presence.

Progressing in our expressions of worship to God will be more difficult for some than others, depending on the cultural and traditional baggage we have to work through; but that's why it is called a "sacrifice." To progress to the place where we are obedient to every prompting of God's Spirit in expressing our love to Him with our body may take a while for some of us, especially if we hold on to any rebellion. But I am convinced that the quicker we get to the place where we can respond to the Spirit's leadership with any biblical expression of worship He asks for, the more fulfilled we will be in every part of our lives. For we will then be functioning the way we were designed to function, for which there is no substitute.

Chapter 8

The Function of the Soul in Worship

The Human Soul

In Chapter Two of this book, I introduced you to the three parts of the human soul. Permit me at this time to share with you Watchman Nee's definition of our soul.

> *"For the seat and essence of the personality is the soul. To comprehend a man's personality is to comprehend his person. Man's existence, characteristics, and life are all in the soul. The Bible consequently calls man a soul. That which constitutes man's personality are the three main faculties of volition, mind, and emotions."*[48]

As a visual reminder, here is the chart I shared in Chapter Two, which shows the three parts of man and the three part of man's soul.

The Worshiper's Anthropology Chart #4 The Soul

1 Thessalonians 5:23	spirit	soul	body
	Will	Mind	Emotions

Table IX

[48] Nee, *Spiritual Man*, 36.

Short Circuits

Our soul is the conductor of our being. Not as in a train or orchestra conductor but rather the electrical conductors.

In the natural world, we have discovered that copper wire is a great conductor of electricity because it provides the least amount of resistance for the cost. Copper wire transfers the power from the source to where it can be useful in light bulbs or appliances. That electrical power is expressed in many different ways, because the conductor allows the power from the source to flow safely and reasonably unhindered to the connected application.

Too often we use our soul as a diffusing filter rather than as a conductor. This means that what is being initiated by our Spirit becomes tainted by our unregenerated soul. Therefore, we end up expressing ourselves with wrong emotions, wrong thought patterns, and wrong choices—emotions, mind, and will. These are what I call "short circuits" in our conductor. Short circuits diffuse the Spirit's initiations in such a way that they disqualify our expressions, even though they may be biblical expressions. Here's the way Paul said it when writing to the Corinthians

> *Though I speak with the tongues of men and of angels, but have not love, I have become sounding brass or a clanging cymbal. And though I have the gift of prophecy, and understand all mysteries and all knowledge, and though I have all faith, so that I could remove mountains, but have not love, I am nothing. And though I bestow all my goods to feed the poor, and though I give my body to be burned, but have not love, it profits me nothing. 1 Corinthians 13:1–3 NKJV*

Just so you understand, love is more than an emotion or feeling. We are supposed to love even when we don't feel like it. Sometimes we are expected to have love as a state-of-mind regardless of how we feel. Likewise, there are times when we must choose to love and forgive, even though it is the last thing we feel like doing. The mind, will, and emotions must all be in harmony for any expression of worship or service we do to be acceptable to God.

All of these acts Paul has listed in the scripture above were intended to bring glory to God when they were initiated by the Holy Spirit. However, all of these physical acts of service and worship were disqualified because of the soul's condition. It doesn't matter how good you do something or what you do, when you have a wrong heart attitude, your expression is disqualified.

A healthy Christian functions this way: the Spirit gives instructions to the soul, the soul obeys the Spirit and has the body carry out the Spirit's instructions.

If you recall, we learned in high school health classes how our brain controls every muscle in our body. We can't even scratch our nose without our mind telling our arm muscles how to get our finger to its target. Then our brain must tell our muscles how to make our finger move back and forth in such a way that we successfully scratch the itch.

Our body is completely controlled by our mind/soul, which is the reason why the Spirit must tell the soul what to have the body do. The Spirit does not control the body directly—the soul controls the body. Unfortunately, the soul or mind has been accustomed to getting its instructions from itself or the body's desires, not from the Spirit. Also, our flesh does not give up its influence on our being without a fight.

What we are describing is the "flow" or "current" of divine inspiration coming from the Spirit of God (which is one with our spirit), through the soul, so it can be expressed by our body. In other words, the spiritually electrified heart of God must be "conducted" by our soul for us to purely express with our body what God initiates by the spirit. Therefore, all three parts of mankind are vitally necessary for us to fulfill our purpose for being created—to be "to the praise of His glory."[49] This is what it means to be led by the Spirit.[50]

---

[49] Eph. 1:14.
[50] Rom. 8:14.

Preparing Our Soul to Conduct Our Worship

Our soul needs to allow what the Spirit of Christ is initiating on the inside of us to flow through it unhindered. For this to happen, our soul, of which our mind is the major part, must be regenerated or renewed. This takes place as we allow the Spirit of Truth, by the Word of Truth, to teach us. To the degree that we have been taught of the Lord is the degree that our mind has been renewed into the image of Christ. This is also the degree that the energized instructions of the Spirit will be applied and expressed by our body.

> *Therefore, I urge you, brothers, in view of God's mercy, to offer your bodies as living sacrifices, holy and pleasing to God—this is your spiritual act of worship. Do not conform any longer to the pattern of this world, but be transformed by the renewing of your mind. Then you will be able to test and approve what God's will is—his good, pleasing and perfect will. Romans 12:1–2 NIV*

Paul, here, is talking about our "spiritual act of worship," which will require that our bodies become sacrifices, not doing what they want to do or what our soul wants them to do, but rather what is good, pleasing, and perfect to God, which the Holy Spirit initiates.

The Worshiper's Anthropology Chart #12

Bible Reference	The Responsibility of our Parts in Worship		
1 Thessalonians 5:23	spirit	soul	body
1 Corinthians 12:3	initiator		
Romans 10:9–10			expresser
Romans 12:2		conductor	

Table XX

To get to the place in our worship where our soul does not short circuit what is being initiated in our spirit, our mind and soul must cease thinking like the world thinks and must be changed according to Christ's mind.

Notice Paul's warning against culture and traditional influences of the world concerning our worship.

> *Do not conform any longer to the pattern of this world,*
> *but be transformed by the renewing of your mind. . . .*
> *Romans 12:2a NIV*

We are told here that the only way to escape being trapped in the world's influences on our worship is to be taught by the Spirit of Truth and the Word of Truth. A literal translation of this warning could read, "Don't let the world squeeze you into its mold or ways of expressing worship."

The word "transformed" here in Greek is *metamorphoo* [met-am-or-fo'-o] (Strong's Greek Number 3339).[51] It literally means to be completely changed from one thing to another. We see this Greek word as the foundation of our English word "metamorphosis," which not only refers to this total and complete change from one thing to another, but it also carries with it the idea that this change is done through a specific process, requiring a specific length of time.

For instance, every chicken was once an egg. Whereas very early sonograms of a developing human child will reveal the resemblance of that developing embryo to the human form, this is not the case with the chicken egg. What's inside the egg at first does not resemble in the least what comes out of the egg after twenty-one days. A chicken has gone through a metamorphosis to become a chicken. It has been changed over a period of time, through a specific, predictable process, from one thing to another. In the 1970s, Barry McGuire sang, "Bullfrogs and butterflies have both been born again." He was speaking of this natural process we call metamorphosis and likening it to the spiritual process of the salvation of our soul.

To be transformed into the image of Christ in our soul requires a

---

[51] Strong, *Strong's Concordance.*

process, which also requires a specific time frame. For the Christian, we will continually be changed in our soul as long as we are on this earth.

> *Being confident of this very thing, that he which hath begun a good work in you will perform it until the day of Jesus Christ: Philippians 1:6 KJV*

The "day of Jesus Christ" is also called the day of "adoption"[52] and refers to the day Jesus will return to Earth for His bride.

God's Perfect Will

Being changed into the image of Christ is the prerequisite for knowing and walking in God's will for our lives. Let's read this again.

> *Do not conform any longer to the pattern of this world, but be transformed by the renewing of your mind. Then you will be able to test and approve what God's will is—his good, pleasing and perfect will. Romans 12:2 NIV*

In the old King James version, the last part of this scripture reads this way.

> *. . . that ye may prove what is that good, and acceptable, and perfect, will of God. Romans 12:2b KJV*

Because of the way this reads, many people have misinterpreted this portion of scripture. I have heard many Bible teachers teach that there is a progression or different levels to God's will. They teach that there is first the "good" will of God, which is the entry level into God's will. Then, they teach that there is an "acceptable" level of God's will, which is what God allows, but it is not the best level of God's will for our lives. Then, finally they teach there is a "perfect" will of God for each person, which we all need to discover. Because of this misinterpretation of this scripture, many have started substituting the word "permissive" for the

---

[52] Rom. 8:23.

word "acceptable" in this scripture. Such liberties with the Word of God can get us into big trouble and lead us into grave deception.

In actuality, these are three adjectives describing the very same thing. In other words, the perfect will of God for our lives is also what is good for us, and it is the only will of God that is acceptable or pleasing to God on our behalf.

By the way, the perfect will of God, according to this scripture, is to present our bodies as sacrifices *to God* as the expresser of our worship of God. Yet, Paul tells us this won't happen unless our soul is renewed, which is the only way to ensure that what our spirit initiates will be allowed to be conveyed through our soul to be expressed by our body. And this spiritual act of worship *is* the perfect, acceptable, and good will of God for our lives.

In the 1960s, Campus Crusade for Christ published its infamous little gold booklet entitled the *Four Spiritual Laws*. Once I accepted Christ in DaNang, Vietnam, in 1970, I used that booklet almost exclusively to lead dozens of soldiers to the Lord in the DaNang Aerial Port. I remember opening the booklet to the first "spiritual law" so many times that I have it memorized. "God loves you and has a wonderful plan for your life." This was the way the first law read from 1965 through 2006. In 2007 it was changed to read "God loves you and offers a wonderful plan for your life."[53]

My hook question following this first law was always, "Wouldn't you want to know what God's plan for your life is?" It would take an idiot to say no to that question, so when they always answered "yes" to it, that gave me the liberty to go through the rest of the four spiritual laws with them and lead them to the Lord.

It was in 1972 when I heard a New Zealander by the name of Winkey Pratney challenge this spiritual law as being unbiblical for the very first time. In his sermon entitled "The Babylonian Pattern," which he preached at the Bethel Assembly of God Church in Wichita, Kansas, he said this:

---

[53] Bright, Bill, *Have You Heard the Four Spiritual Laws?* (Peachtree, GA: Bright Media Foundation and Campus Crusade for Christ, 2007). https://crustore.org/downloads/4laws.pdf

"For years I've preached that 'God loves you and has a wonderful plan for your life.' We preachers have a tendency to preach things that we don't know where they are in the Bible, so I thought I had better look it up, so I would have a scripture reference to back up what I was preaching. The problem is I couldn't find the word 'plan' in scripture to support this concept. So, I looked up the word 'blueprint' and couldn't find it either. What I did find was the word 'purpose.'"

And we know that all things work together for good to them that love God, to them who are the called according to his purpose. Romans 8:28 KJV

"What makes the game of football so interesting," Winkey continued, "is the opposing team is trying to gain possession of the ball and take it to the goal so they can score points and hopefully win the game. In the game of football, the goal does not change or move about. However, every few seconds the 'plan' changes. God doesn't have 'a' plan for your life; God has a 'purpose' for your life. If your football team shows up to a game with only one play, when you start getting the stuffing beat out of you, because the opposing team has figured out your plan, you better change the plan."[54]

What is the purpose of life? Let me remind you.

Having made known unto us the mystery of his will, according to his good pleasure which he hath purposed in himself: That in the dispensation of the fullness of times he might gather together in one all things in Christ, both which are in heaven, and which are on earth; even in him: In whom also we have obtained an inheritance, being predestinated according to the purpose of him who worketh all things after the counsel of his own will: That we should be to the praise of his glory, who first trusted in Christ. Ephesians 1:9–12 KJV

---

[54] Pratney, Winky. The Babylonian Pattern. (1972). Retrieved 2016.

Our goal is to be to the praise of His glory. That is our purpose. The devil wants us to get locked into plans, so he can beat us up. But God is always changing the play to keep the devil off guard. There is not a specific plan or will of God for your life. There is a specific purpose or goal. How we reach that goal doesn't matter. It only matters that we reach the goal and that everything we do and every step we take (being ordered of God[55]) is to cause us to reach the goal.

> *Whether therefore ye eat, or drink, or whatsoever ye do,*
> *do all to the glory of God. 1 Corinthians 10:31 KJV*

In other words, whatever you do, let it be done with the purpose or goal in mind of giving glory to God. This is God's will for you. It doesn't matter if you are a teacher or a garbage collector in life. All that matters is whether you are a worshiper. That is God's will for your life!

> *Rejoice evermore. Pray without ceasing. In everything*
> *give thanks: for this is the will of God in Christ Jesus*
> *concerning you. 1 Thessalonians 5:16–18 KJV*

In everything, whatever you do, being a worshiper is God's will for you. Do what you want to do in life, just make sure it facilitates you accomplishing your purpose, reaching your goal, doing God's will of being a worshiper!

Our Worship of God Is Our Service to God

In the King James version, our worship is called our "reasonable service."

> *I beseech you therefore, brethren, by the mercies of*
> *God, that ye present your bodies a living sacrifice, holy,*
> *acceptable unto God, which is your reasonable service.*
> *Romans 12:1 KJV*

---

[55] Ps. 37:23.

There are two very important things to point out here. First of all, it is not unreasonable for us to worship God according to His Spirit, even if it means our body and soul must be sacrificed for this to be accomplished.

Second, our worship of God is our service to God. When we serve someone, we are ministering to his or her needs, not our own needs. A true servant does not think of him- or herself first but rather thinks of how he or she may meet the needs of those he or she is serving.

Although God is completely independent and needs nothing from any other being, God has chosen to need our worship by creating us with worship as the sole purpose for our existence. Therefore, as we serve God with our worship, we should be only mindful of what will bless Him, not us. Our comfort is less than of secondary concern when it comes to meeting God's need to be praised. Therefore, it is only reasonable that our desires, our comfort, and the benefits we receive when worshipping the Lord are not considered when we worship. Our attitude motivating us to worship and sustaining us during the act of worship must be that we only want to please the Almighty God.

In 1983, I attended one of the original Worship Symposiums in Pasadena, California. I remember boarding a shuttle bus with people from all around the world who had come to attend that conference. On the bus, I overheard a conversation between two of the conference delegates. This conversation has stuck with me all this time. They were speaking with great anticipation about the opening gathering to the conference that evening. One stated how she knew it would be an awesome time in the presence of God, but the other woman kept saying how much she needed to worship God and how she was starting to experience withdrawal symptoms because it had been several days since she had worshiped, meaning in a corporate setting.

Let me interject this thought before I finish my story. Before there can be dynamic corporate worship, we as individuals must develop a personal worship lifestyle. If we have to be with other people to worship Jesus, something's wrong.

I listened intently for her to focus her desires on the Lord Jesus, but she never did. Instead, she continued to lift up worship as the focus.

She did not put her focus on the object of her worship—Jesus. Both women's focuses were on themselves and what they expected to get out of the corporate worship experience that night. They were more concerned with what worship could do for them, rather than who they were worshipping and what would bring Him pleasure.

Over the years, I have met many people just like this person who were addicted to worship or at least to the benefits they received from corporately worshipping God. The benefits that we experience by entering into the presence of God are tremendous. However, that should never become our motivation for worshipping God. These benefits should only remain the results of our worship, not the reason for it. Otherwise, our emphasis is on us and what we want and need, rather than on Christ and what He wants and needs. This wrong attitude makes it difficult for us to think of our worship as a continual sacrifice and the putting to death of our desires. Then, when the Spirit of God initiates an expression of worship from us that we are uncomfortable with, we consider it would be wrong to express our worship in that way, since it makes us uncomfortable.

More recently a popular Christian song, which has received a lot of airplay on Christin radio stations, contains the line "I'm about to get my worship on."[56] It's a great song, but again, it is written from the perspective of "I" and "my," not who He is and what He has done to deserve our worship.

My good friend Lamar Boschman[57] coined the phrase "Transcendent Worship," which he defines as worship that is focused on the Lord, not ourselves. That kind of worship transcends this earthly perspective of "me" and enlarges our God, who becomes our total focus in our worship.

Worship should never revolve around us and what we want—it should always revolve around Jesus and how He wants us to express our love to Him.

---

[56] Grace, J., T. McKeehan, M. Nichols, C. Stevens, *Beautiful Day*, Capitol CMG, 2013, compact disc.

[57] Founder of the International Worship Institute.

Results of Our Worship

What are some of the results of our worship when our entire being is in tune with the Holy Spirit's initiation of worship? Isaiah gives a tremendous list of these results.

To read the book of Isaiah, it becomes apparent that there are times when Isaiah has not written anything for a while and then goes into a new topic, having received fresh revelation from the Lord. Such a break occurs at Chapter 60, and the new topic on God's heart is worship. Isaiah bursts into this subject declaring the commandment of the Lord for us to "rise and shine!"

> *Arise, shine; for thy light is come, and the glory of the Lord is risen upon thee. Isaiah 60:1 KJV*

In *Biblical Worship*,[58] we studied many of the Greek and Hebrew words that have been translated into the various Bible synonyms of the word "worship." We learned that the Hebrew word *halal*, which is translated "praise" in English, can mean "to shine." Therefore, this commandment for us to "Arise, shine" could be said like this: "Get up and praise the Lord!" If we obey this commandment, Isaiah lists some things we can expect to happen as the result of our praising God.

> *And the Gentiles shall come to thy light, and kings to the brightness of thy rising. Lift up thine eyes round about, and see: all they gather themselves together, they come to thee: thy sons shall come from far, and thy daughters shall be nursed at thy side.*
> *Then thou shalt see, and flow together, and thine heart shall fear, and be enlarged; because the abundance of the sea shall be converted unto thee, the forces of the Gentiles shall come unto thee. Isaiah 60:3–5 KJV*

---

[58] Stone, *Biblical Worship*, Chapter Four.

The first result of true biblical worship is people will be drawn to "the brightness of thy rising." It will include both common folk and nobility. They will all come to see who you are so in love with that you would sacrifice your living body in worship to express your love to Him. I call this "worship evangelism." A true worshipper will have many spiritual sons and daughters that he or she is nurturing in the Lord. This doesn't happen because we set a goal to share Christ with so many people each week. It happens because we have obeyed the commandment to get up and praise God! When talking with his disciples about being raised up on the cross to die, Jesus even prophesied that this would happen to his disciples.

> *And I, if I be lifted up from the earth, will draw all men unto me. John 12:32 KJV*

This scripture, like many others, has layers of meanings. Not only did Jesus mean He would be lifted up on the cross, but also that every time we worship Jesus we are lifting Him high above the things of this earth. We are recognizing Him as the one and only true and living God. When we do this, He will draw *all* who come to Him. No one will come to Christ and have a lasting relationship with Him because of our skills of persuasion. All God needs is for us to function the way He designed us to function, and His glory on us will draw others to Himself.

The rest of the results of worship that Isaiah listed in this chapter benefit the individual worshiper. "Then thou shalt see" refers to a greater level of spiritual understanding. "And flow together" talks about a level of corporate unity that catapults us into a dimension where nothing is impossible.

> *The Lord said, "If as one people speaking the same language they have begun to do this, then nothing they plan to do will be impossible for them." Genesis 11:6 NIV*

"Thine heart shall fear" brings further results and changes within the individual worshiper, because "The fear of the Lord is the beginning of wisdom. . ."[59] "And thine heart shall. . . be enlarged" refers to an

---

[59] Prov. 9:10 (KJV).

increased capacity within the worshiper to feel what God feels. We begin to understand what it felt like for Jesus to be "moved with compassion."[60]

These are just a few of the biblical results of worship. We will discuss more of the benefits of corporate worship in the next book in this series, *Corporate Worship.*

A Definition of Worship

Worship is the expression of our love to God, which the Holy Spirit initiates inside us, being conducted through our soul so that our body might express it in obedience to the Spirit and the Word of Truth.

The Soul Conformed to Christ's Image

Permit me to revisit this topic at this time. God made man like Himself in two ways: in His likeness and in His image.[61] God's Image refers to His character, not His form. When Adam and Eve sinned in the Garden of Eden, their souls eventually became dead by the influence of the curse of sin, which is death. Adam and Eve did not lose the likeness of God in their bodies, but their bodies died. They did lose the character of God in their personalities. A person's personality has its "seat" within the three parts of the soul—emotions, mind, and will. We define a person's personality by his or her thought processes (mind), displayed feelings (emotions), and what he or she chooses to do (will).[62] Our personality is intertwined with our character.

Because Adam and Eve sinned, every human born on the earth has been born reflecting a satanic image or character in our personality. If you don't believe me, spend a day at a preschool in a class of children who are not used to being around other children. Knowing how to share is something each child must learn. Some learn it quicker than others, and some never learn it. Where did all that selfish action and self-centered attitude come from? Every human is born with it, because of Adam and Eve.

---

[60] Matt. 14:14.

[61] Gen. 1:26.

[62] Nee, *Spiritual Man.*

As it is written, There is none righteous, no, not one:
Romans 3:10 KJV

We are speaking of our soul here, not our spirit. Our spirit has been made one with God's Spirit, if we have confessed Jesus as our Lord.[63] Our soul needs the character of Christ formed in us, which is the same thing as us being conformed into Christ's image or character.

For whom He foreknew, He also predestined to be conformed to the image of His Son, that He might be the firstborn among many brethren. Romans 8:29 NKJV

Because our soul was born with a sin nature, it must be reprogrammed to think like Jesus thinks, feel like Jesus feels, and chose our actions like Jesus would. This is what we call our soul being conformed into Christ's image.

How do we know that the image of Christ is being formed in us? It is by the fruit our lives bare. There is a description in scripture of God's character that we can hold up next to our personality to see how much of God's image has been formed in us. Here is that list.

But the fruit of the Spirit is love, joy, peace, longsuffering, kindness, goodness, faithfulness, gentleness, self-control. Against such there is no law. Galatians 5:22–23 NKJV

I believe we should think of this list in this way first.

Galatians 5:22-23 Applied to Our Soul

Emotions	Mind	Will
love	longsuffering	faithfulness
joy	kindness	gentleness
peace	goodness	self-control

Table XXI

---

[63] Rom. 10:9–10.

There are nine character traits that are evidence that God's image is being formed in our personality, which is our soul. The first three character traits apply first to our emotions. Love, joy, and peace are the three significant positive human emotions.

The second three Godly character traits on this list are applied first to our mental attitudes to reflect Christ's character. God wants us to walk in an attitude of forgiveness so that, no matter what takes place in our lives, we will always forgive. This means we will suffer as long as it takes, because that is who Christ has made us to be by His Spirit. Likewise, acts of kindness and goodness come from a renewed mindset of serving others first. This becomes who we are (in Christ). It is the person God has made us to be by the working of His Holy Spirit and the Word of God in our lives.

The last three character traits in this list represent areas that require our will to resolve to do them as we find ourselves engaged in various life situations. In life, we will always be tempted to give into our flesh, to not be faithful, to not be gentle, and to not control ourselves, especially when we feel justified in following our fallen nature. In the heat of the moment, it is always easier to give up, lose control, and really let someone "have it." It is only by Christ's character being formed in us over time that our will is empowered in that moment to do the right things.

Christ's character is established in our soul "line upon line"[64] as we "grow in the grace and the knowledge"[65] of our Lord Jesus Christ, and the way we know God's character/image is being formed in us is when we see these nine evidences in operation in our day-to-day lives.

The Struggle Over Christ's Image

Not only are we battling against our flesh to have the image of Christ formed in us, but Satan hates the image of God's character being formed in us as well. He hates the character of God and wants to destroy it. Yet, he knows he does not have enough power to attack God directly,

---

[64] Is. 28:9–10.
[65] 2 Pet. 3:18.

so he attacks God's image in us by attacking our soul. He attacks God's likeness in us by attacking our body.

In *Biblical Worship*,[66] we learned that the two sins that got Lucifer kicked out of heaven were 1) wanting to be like the Most High God and 2) wanting to receive worship for himself.

In response to those sins, God banished Lucifer to the earth. There God proceeded to create mankind as punishment for Lucifer's sins. For Lucifer's first sin of wanting to be like God, He created an entire species in His own likeness and image so Lucifer will forever be reminded, every time he looks at one of us, of that sin and that he will never be like God in any way.

For the second sin of Lucifer desiring worship for himself, he lost his job in heaven as the primary worship leader. We will study Lucifer as the heavenly worship leader in depth in the next two books of this series, *Corporate Worship* and *Leading Worship*. For now, simply understand that God created Lucifer to be one of the three highest-ranking angels in heaven. The title God gave these angels was archangel.[67] The angel Gabriel is in charge of communications. Michel commands the waring angels. Lucifer was the heavenly worship leader and was created with that specific job in mind.

To punish Lucifer for desiring worship for himself, God made the primary purpose of mankind to be worshipers of the Most High. God also made our worship of Him as painful to Lucifer as a two-edged sword is to us. Then God instructed mankind that it would be our privilege and honor to execute His judgments against Lucifer as we worship the Lord.

> *Let the high praises of God be in their mouth, And (which is) a two-edged sword in their hand, To execute vengeance on the nations (kingdom of Satin), And punishments on the peoples (demons); To bind their kings (principalities) with chains, And their nobles (powers) with fetters of iron; To execute on them the written judgment—This honor have all His saints. Praise the Lord! Psalm 149:6–9 NKJV*

---

[66] Stone, *Biblical Worship*, Chapter Eight.

[67] 1 Thess. 4:16.

Our worship of our creator is what punishes the devil for his sins. It cuts him, and his demons, like a two-edged sword. It binds them with chains and fetters of iron. It carries out God's written judgment and sentencing on Lucifer. For a better knowledge of these written judgements, read Chapter Eight of *Biblical Worship*.

To keep us from executing the judgments written against Lucifer found in Isaiah Chapter 14, Satan goes on the offensive. Satan attacks every Christian in the two areas God intended for mankind to be like Himself: His image and His likeness. Satan attacks God's likeness in us with sickness and infirmity. Satan attacks God's image in us with implanted ungodly thoughts, imaginations, and temptations. Satan attacks God's likeness in us by attacking our body. Satan attacks God's image in us by attacking our soul.

A Christian's spirit is off limits to satanic attack because the Holy Spirit has been joined to our spirit. That leaves only our unregenerated soul and decaying body as targets for the devil to attack.

Chapter 9

Understanding Our Soul

Natural Understanding

It is now time to revisit this topic. All three parts of our soul are processed in our brain. Our brain is like a computer, which is programmed to create files for every event or experience we have in our lives. We also create files for every relationship we have or every person we know or know about. We will discuss these people files in the next book *Corporate Worship*, but we will discuss the experience files here.

While we are going through an experience, our brains keep every detail about that experience in our file, because it is difficult to fully process the experience in the midst of it and determine which data is important to keep or discard.

However, every experience we go through requires us to continually analyze all the data we are receiving about the current experience, because most experiences in life are interactive. We must continually analyze the data we are receiving to plot our next move or words.

The natural data we receive in every experience comes from our five senses. The questions we are always on alert to answer in every experience we have are these.

1. What are we seeing here in this experience?
2. What are we hearing here in this experience?

3. What are we physically feeling in this experience?
4. What are the tastes of this experience?
5. What are the smells of this experience?

Every time we enter data from the five senses into a current event file in our mind, we piece the puzzle of that event together using that data to help us reach these three conclusions about that experience. These conclusions correlate with the three parts of our soul.

1. What cognitive conclusions can we derive from this event or entry? Another way of asking this question would be: What do we *think* about this event or entry?
2. What do our emotions register from this event or entry? Or, what do we *feel* (emotionally) about this event or entry?
3. What is the best course of action, if any, that we should take because of this event or entry? Or, what will we *do* about this event or entry?

This is the way we arrive at natural understanding.

Natural Understanding

Bible Reference	The Parts of a Human Being		
1 Thessalonians 5:23	spirit	soul	body
1 Corinthians 14:15	spirit	understanding	

Table XXII

Natural understanding comes from processing data from our five senses and our fleshly emotions. Spiritual understanding comes from processing data from the Spirit (which the Word of Truth will validate) and our emotions when they are reflecting the feelings of the Spirit. Our "natural man" cannot understand our Spirit without the Holy Spirit's help.

> *But the natural man receiveth not the things of the Spirit of God: for they are foolishness unto him: neither can*

he know them, because they are spiritually discerned. 1 Corinthians 2:14 KJV

What Are Our Emotions?

The way we stay in touch with the physical part of our being is through our five senses transmitting data to the brain through our nervous system. The way we stay in touch with our soul, and sometimes our Spirit, is through our emotions. The emotions indicate the status of the nonphysical parts of our being in the same way the senses and the nervous system indicate the status of the physical part of our being. Therefore, we call the emotions the "indicators." Please keep in mind that all three functions of our soul (mind, will, and emotions) are processed in our mind or brain.

To understand what the emotions are, think of them as meters. Each meter reports on a different inner feeling, or emotion, and contributes to the overall category of emotions it is in. Our emotional indicators are like this picture of a meter.

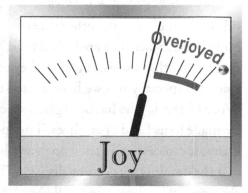

Joy Meter

When the meter indicating joy in our being is not registering or the needle is all the way to the left, there is an absence of joy in our being. When the needle begins to bobble to the right, it means joy is registering. The more joy we have, the higher the needle rises to the right toward the red zone. Once the needle is into the red zone, we are overjoyed or extremely joyful. It is possible to also peg this type of meter. That's when the needle stays far to the right without movement and stays there in such a way that it is impossible to determine exactly how much joy you are experiencing. That is called being "pegged" because the needle lays against a peg at the right edge of the red zone, keeping it from breaking off inside the meter.

The person whose joy meter is shown above is very full of joy right now but not yet extremely full of joy. That person is getting close, though.

The Will Is Chairman of the Board

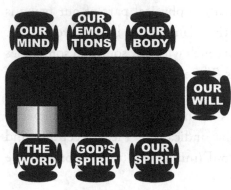

Our Being Making a Decision

As you know, a chairman of the board only votes when the board is tied. Picture a board room. Seated around the table are the parts of our being, with our will occupying the head chair. On the right side of the table sits our body. Next to the body is our emotions, and finally our mind is at the end on that side of the table. On the other side of the table is our spirit, joined by the Holy Spirit. Since they are linked together, they both are considered one spirit.[68] In other words, together they only get one vote. Seated with the spirit is a special guest we have invited to weigh in on our decisions, the Word of Truth, who has been given special voting privileges since the day we made Jesus Lord of our lives. The special rule for the Word of Truth is that it can cast more than one vote, but it does not have the ability to cast the deciding vote on any decision. That privilege belongs only to the chairman of the board, our will. Any board member can suggest a course of action for our being and call for a vote on that action.

"Come to order," our will calls out, as it strikes the table with the gavel. "God's Spirit has proposed that we stand up and lift our hands in worship to Almighty God. What say you?"

"Oh man," the body whines. "I am *so* tired! I've been on my feet all day, and they are killing me! My back is hurting, and I think I pulled a muscle in my right shoulder or something. I may be able to hold that hand up halfway for 30 seconds, but I doubt it. I think we ought to sit this one out, so I can rest."

---

[68] 1 Cor. 6:17.

"What do you think, emotions?" our will asks.

"Well," the emotions begin, "I'm very uncomfortable with any demonstrative expression! That's just not me at all! If the young people want to do it, that's fine, but I get really embarrassed expressing myself in ways I am uncomfortable doing. After all, I've always been shy—that's just the way I am. Furthermore, I am offended to think you want me to do something outside my comfort zone. My vote is with the body! We should sit this one out!"

"Well," our will summarizes, "that's one for and two against. Does the mind have anything else to add?"

The mind begins to review the event file in a computerized monotone. "The body is tired. The feet hurt. The back hurts. The right shoulder hurts and is weak. The emotions are uncomfortable, embarrassed, shy, and offended.,"

"We all knew those things, Mind," our will responds. "What we want to know is what you think about the Spirit's proposal to stand and lift our hands in worship."

The mind pauses for a moment, then responds. "In searching our memory banks, I can tell you with certainty that we have never expressed worship like that before. We have experienced every one of these emotions before, but none of the experiences were in the context of worship. However, every event file associated with these emotions were extremely unpleasant. Therefore, I concur with the body's counter proposal to sit this one out."

"Well, that's it then." Our will raises the gavel to declare the board's consensus. But before the gavel could hit the table, the Word of God interrupts.

"Excuse Me!" the Word of God declares. "I have something to say about this matter!"

The body rolls its eyes and lets out a heavy sigh. The emotions clench its teeth with anger. The mind opens the event file again, since it closed the file prematurely. Mind picks up a pen to continue taking minutes of the meeting.

"I'm surprised at you, Mind," the Word states. "After all the time I have spent trying to renew you, you did not come up with one scripture to refute Body's and Emotions' arguments. Did you even try, or did you simply let them tell you what to think?" The Word has become passionate at this point. "Let me remind you of what you should be thinking! Romans 12:1 says that the body has *nothing* to say when it comes to worship! It is to be a living sacrifice—that's all! And I don't care if Emotions are uncomfortable with the body raising its hands. 1 Timothy 2:8 in the New King James Version says, 'I desire therefore that men pray (or worship) everywhere, lifting up holy hands, without wrath and doubting.'"

The Word, knowing it has presented the two scriptures required to even the vote, sits back in his chair and waits for our will's decision. "I have much more evidence to present," the Word declares, "and I will gladly give it. But the rules state that you are now faced with the decision. Are you going to obey the flesh or the Spirit?"

The Search Engine

At the same time, our mind is processing every entry in our current event file, conducting the following searches of our memory or knowledge files.

1. Have I ever seen/read anything like this before?
2. Have I ever heard anything like this before?
3. Have I ever physically felt anything like this before?
4. Have I ever tasted anything like this before?
5. Have I ever smelt anything like this before?
6. Have I ever thought this way about an event before?
7. Have my emotions ever registered like this before?
8. Have I ever done before what I am contemplating doing now?

If our search engine comes up with a positive result for any of these questions, the mind quickly scans the processed overall conclusions of that memory file for our consideration in determining or plotting our next words or course of action for the current event.

Here are the conclusions that every processed file a Christian carries should have.

1. Mental conclusions of the event
   a. What did my carnal mind think about the event?
   b. What did my renewed mind think about this event?
2. Emotional feelings of the event
   a. What natural emotions did I feel in this event?
   b. What Godly emotions did I assign to this file?
3. What did I do about this event?
   a. Was my actions or words pleasing to the Spirit or the flesh?
   b. What was the result of my actions or words?
   c. Did I do or say the right thing according to the Word of God?
   d. How do I feel emotionally, both naturally and spiritually, about what I did?
   e. Is this a recommended action for the future?

All this processing, searching, and reviewing goes on in our mind as quickly as we as individuals are capable of. Psychiatrists are able to determine our individual processing speed from tests. For some of us, it can all happen in a fraction of a second. Most of us will take several seconds to several minutes to process things. Others take hours or longer. The more complex the event and the more emotional indicators that are registering, the longer it will take to process that event file. If you process things more slowly than others, *do not* stop trying. You will get somewhat faster at it the more you do it. The important thing is to process every file of every event you experience and store your conclusions at the front of that event file.

If you have not processed an event file, then you will be flooded and overwhelmed with all the raw data of that file when you open it during your search. This can bring you into a state of confusion and stop you from correctly processing the current event file. Then you will have two unprocessed memory files in storage, which will double the possibility of opening an unprocessed memory file in the future. With every unprocessed file, you increase your chances of opening unprocessed files exponentially. Eventually, this will put you—and keep you—in a perpetual state of confusion. After you stay that way long enough, it will present itself as an open door for a spirit of confusion to enter your life. This is possible, even for Christians, because the soul is not yet totally redeemed.

If this has already happened to you, *do not panic*! It is easily fixable! All we have to do is follow God's instructions found in the book of James.

> *Therefore submit to God. Resist the devil and he will flee from you. Draw near to God and He will draw near to you. . . James 4:7–8 KJV*

Based on this "deliverance formula," pray this prayer out loud.

> *Dear Lord Jesus, I choose to submit to You in this area by repenting for allowing unprocessed memory files to exist in my mind. I am sorry for allowing that to happen. Help me to, over time, process every pertinent, unresolved memory file I have. Until that can happen, Lord, I ask that you place a caution sign on every unprocessed file in my memory, so I know not to open it until I am ready to process it, so it will not hinder me from processing any future event files. Thank you, Jesus, for forgiving me for this, and helping me to correct this in the future!*
>
> *Now, devil, you spirit of confusion, and all other spirits you have let in through this open door: The door is now shut by my repentance! You no longer have any legal right to attack me in this area. Therefore, by the authority given to me in Jesus' name, I command all of you to leave me now! Thank you Jesus for enforcing my words!"*

If confusion, or other spirits, ever try to attack you again over this, remind them that their attacks are no longer legal in this area and the door of that stronghold has been shut! If they persist to bang on that closed door, to try to control you again from that stronghold, remind them that you will report them to the righteous Judge for their illegal activity, and the Lord will rebuke them![69] No devil ever wants to be rebuked by our Lord, so it will comply with your demands, as long as you keep that stronghold door closed!

Make today the "first day of the rest of your life," and start today saving every event file, after you have processed it in accordance to the principles of the Word of God and the Holy Spirit's leading. Healthy memories are established by coming to natural and spiritual understanding about every event in life.

The Three Cognitive Functions of the Mind

There are a multitude of subconscious functions of the human brain. For instance, we do not need to think about breathing. This is controlled subconsciously by our brain without a conscious thought. Other subconscious functions of the human brain would include walking, scratching, coughing, sneezing, the beating of our heart, growing, and on and on the list goes.

God programs the subconscious functions of the human brain to sustain or maintain human life. It would be impossible for us to consciously control every heart beat and every breath we take and get anything else done. Thank God, He preprogrammed our brain to deal with all that, so we can use the conscious part of our brain for more important things.

We do not gain much, if anything, by bringing a subconscious function of the brain into the conscious level of our mind. Here's what Jesus said about this by using one subconscious brain function as His example.

> *Which of you by taking thought can add one cubit unto his stature? Matthew 6:27 KJV*

The power of positive thinking never works on things that our subconscious mind, which God preprogrammed, controls. It is the

---

[69] Jude 9.

human mind's conscious functions that we need to examine in this study on worship.

In the following scripture from 2 Corinthians, Paul is teaching us about spiritual warfare. More specifically, Paul is identifying for us where strongholds occur. By telling us this, Paul also reveals to us the human brain's three conscious cognitive functions. It is in the mind where our enemy sets up strongholds as open doors where he can continue to attack us.

> For though we walk in the flesh, we do not war after the flesh: (For the weapons of our warfare are not carnal, but mighty through God to the pulling down of strongholds;) Casting down **imaginations**, and every high thing that exalteth itself against the **knowledge** of God, and bringing into captivity every **thought** to the obedience of Christ; And having in a readiness to revenge all disobedience, when your obedience is fulfilled. 2 Corinthians 10:3–6 KJV, emphasis added

I have chosen to use the King James version of this scripture because several newer translations of the Bible change the word "imaginations," making it difficult for us to understand these three conscious functions of the mind. To summarize, the three cognitive functions of the conscious mind are 1) imaginations, 2) knowledge, and 3) thoughts.

Knowledge is the gaining and storing of data from our five senses in the processed memory files of every event we have had. Unprocessed files are not knowledge. They are only raw data, if we have not learned anything from the experience. Knowledge is one of the main functions of our human "computer"—to store and retrieve data. Every piece of data, as well as every thought we have ever had, is stored in memory in our brain. Every experience we have had in our life is stored in memory files. Every piece of data processed into knowledge we have gained from any media is stored in our brain. This comprises the level of knowledge we have obtained to this point in our life.

Thoughts are cognitive reasonings, conclusions, or deductions that we make based on data we have received. This data may come from our emotions, our five senses, our current experience, our memories of similar experiences, books, television, movies, other media, reports of experiences of other people, etc.

Keep in mind that every decision or thought we think is always based on incomplete information or data. In this life, it is impossible to have all the facts on all levels of information.

For we know in part. . . 1Corinthians 13:9 NKJV

That's why our ability to think and reason is so vital. This is another thing that sets mankind apart from the rest of God's creations—the ability to perform deductive reasoning and reach conclusions without having all the data in any given situation. A computer can think, if you program it to and provide it with all the data necessary with which to think. However, deductive reasoning is impossible for a computer. Only a being created in the image and likeness of God has that ability. In other words, human thoughts are far more advanced than the thoughts of a computer, which must be programmed as to the train of thought it is supposed to follow.

Imaginations are creative thoughts. In other words, imaginations are a particular type of thought. Not all thoughts are imaginations, but all imaginations are thoughts. Every person has imaginative thoughts. Many people have told me they quit using their imagination when they became adults, but that is not true. We all use our imagination, whether we realize it or not.

Here's an example of how we use imagination in our day-to-day lives. As you get out of your car to go into your house, a car pulls up and stops. A passenger in the car rolls down his window and asks for directions to a particular place. Your brain quickly searches your memory banks, and you realize you know right where the place is that he wants to go to. The next thing you do is begin to imagine going to the place yourself. As you imagine the journey, you describe for the person how to get there. Most of the time, the person receiving the directions has to remember the information only as data. The only exception to this is when the person is familiar with any landmarks or streets you are describing to him. In that case, he can also begin to remember and imagine that part of the journey as well.

Every building or house we live in or work in had to start as someone's imagination. Every invention we enjoy that makes our lives better or easier started as an imagination. We all use our imaginations all the time.

Try this exercise. After you read this paragraph of instructions, close your eyes to follow the instructions, so you will not be distracted by things you see. First, imagine the front of your house or the building where you live. Now imagine the back of that structure. Next imagine one of the sides, then the other side. Now imagine you are rising up above your house or building and looking down on it.

Only less than 1 percent of people struggle to imagine the top of their living facility, even though most of us have never seen it from that vantage point.

Did you know that our body and emotions cannot tell the difference between imaginations and reality? Imagine that you are standing in my kitchen with me and we are talking. As we talk, I go to the refrigerator and pull out a big gallon jar of dill pickles, open it, fish out a five-inch-long pickle with a fork, and hand it to you. Not wanting to offend my hospitality, you take the pickle and take a big bite of it.

Even as you read this last paragraph your saliva glands began to prepare your mouth for the taste of a dill pickle, because your body and emotions cannot tell the difference between reality and imaginations.

Here is a scripture from 1 Chronicles, which also refers to these three functions of the human mind—knowledge, thoughts, and imaginations. It is these three functions of our mind—our cognitive skills—that set mankind apart from the rest of creation.

> *And thou, Solomon my son, **know** thou the God of thy father, and serve him with a perfect heart and with a willing mind: for the LORD searcheth all hearts, and understandeth all the **imaginations** of the **thoughts**: if thou seek him, he will be found of thee; but if thou forsake him, he will cast thee off forever. 1 Chronicles 28:9 KJV, emphasis added*

The Three Levels of Trichotomy

1 Thessalonians 5:23	spirit	soul	body
	Will	Mind	Emotions
	Imaginations	Knowledge	Thoughts

Table XXIII

What Are Strongholds?

Since we mentioned strongholds, let me share a couple of things about them that might help you. Here is a quick overview.

According to 2 Corinthians 10:3–5, Strongholds occur in the three conscience functions of our mind: knowledge, thoughts, and imaginations. Strongholds are formed in our mind when we accept a lie as truth.

Since our mind is not yet totally redeemed, the devil has access to our mind, as do we and God. What the devil does with our knowledge and event files is to suggest wrong or carnal conclusions. If we accept these conclusions as truth, that mental knowledge file becomes a legal stronghold, or "open door," for the devil to attack us through in the future. This is why it is so important to process every file in light of the Word of God. Remember, your flesh is the enemy of truth. Every thought and imagination must be examined in light of the Word of God to guard against the devil establishing another stronghold in our mind.

The question that comes after learning this is what do we do if we suspect we have believed lies from the devil? The answer is found in this scripture.

> And the servant of the Lord must not strive; but be gentle
> unto all men, apt to teach, patient, In meekness instructing
> those that oppose themselves; if God peradventure will
> give them repentance to the acknowledging of the truth;

And that they may recover themselves out of the snare of the devil, who are taken captive by him at his will. 2 Timothy 2:24–26 KJV

First, go to a trusted, mature Christian who knows the Word of God. Ask him or her about the conclusions, thoughts, and imaginations you are unsure of. Listen to them and don't argue! When you have believed a lie, you are actually opposing yourself. Your spirit-man desires truth in the inward parts,[70] yet your carnal man has embraced a lie.

If you have believed a lie, then you must do two things: "repentance to the acknowledging of the truth" and "recover yourself out of the snare of the devil, who are taken captive by him at his will."

True Biblical deliverance is not someone commanding an evil spirit to leave you. It is you recovering yourself from Satan's grip by rejecting his lies and declaring God's truth!

*And ye shall know the truth, and the truth shall **make** you free. John 8:32 KJV, emphasis added*

This is one of the most misquoted verses in the Bible. Everyone I know says the truth will "set" you free. But that's not what the scripture says. To be set free implies the concept of deliverance, where we have nothing to do with our freedom. Somebody else has to come along and unlocked our jail cell. This belief supports the type of deliverance pattern where people gather around a person and yell at the demons, commanding them to get out!

This type of activity never brings lasting deliverance. At best it brings only temporary relief to the one being tormented. True enduring deliverance only comes when a person recovers him- or herself by renouncing the lies he or she has believed and acknowledging the truth. When we do this, the truth "makes" us free.

---

[70] Ps. 51:6.

Three Categories of Pleasurable Emotions

In the last chapter, we looked at Galatians 5:22–23 as to how it applies to the image of Christ being formed in our soul. This same scripture gives us the three categories of pleasurable human emotions. Let me show you what I mean. Flip back to Table XXI, and review it so you have that image in your mind. Now mentally eliminate the heading row – Emotions, Mind, and Will. Next take the bottom left-

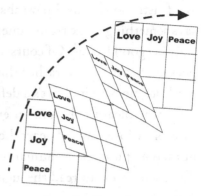

Love Joy Peace bottom left to top right

hand corner and make it the top right-hand corner like this, leaving Love, Joy, Peace as the new heading row. Here's the way our chart looks now.

Galatians 5:22-23 Applied to Our Emotions

Love	Joy	Peace
longsuffering	*kindness*	*goodness*
faithfulness	*gentleness*	*self-control*

Table XXIV

Now think of the new heading row as not only a positive-type of emotion but also what you would like to see others around you find (or know)—Love, Joy, and Peace. The greatest heart motivation for ourselves is love;[71] therefore, all of the remaining six Godly character traits are expressions of love on our part toward our fellow man. But if we want others to know love, the two most important things we can do for them is walk in forgiveness toward them—which is long suffering— and remain faithful to them at all cost. If our heart motivation is for someone to know the joy of the Lord, we treat him or her with kindness and gentleness. Nothing steals a person's joy faster than unkindness and

---

[71] 1 Cor. 13:13.

harshness. Likewise, if we want someone to have peace, we do everything in our power to do good for that individual and not let him or her see any frustrations in us. I have absolutely no peace when someone does or says something to me from a questionable heart attitude or motive of not wanting good for me. Of course, I would rather wonder about the other person's heart motive rather than have the individual lose control and really let me have it. That's a definite peace-stealer.

Every pleasurable human emotion will fit into one of these three categories: love, joy, and peace. Let me show you what I mean. I have listed numerous pleasurable human emotions under these three categories. Take some time to read through these lists so you can understand this concept.

Emotions of Pleasure

Love	Joy	Peace
1. absorbed	1. alive	1. accepted
2. admiration	2. amazed	2. accepting
3. adoration	3. amusement	3. amazement
4. affection	4. astonishment	4. at ease
5. attraction	5. bliss	5. blessed
6. bold	6. bright	6. calm
7. brave	7. cheerfulness	7. certain
8. caring	8. clever	8. comfortable
9. comforted	9. curious	9. confident
10. compassion	10. delighted	10. content
11. considerate	11. delightful	11. contentment
12. courageous	12. eagerness	12. hope
13. daring	13. ecstatic	13. important
14. desire	14. elation	14. open
15. determined	15. encouraged	15. optimism
16. devoted	16. energetic	16. peaceful
17. drawn toward	17. enjoyment	17. pleasure
18. dynamic	18. enthusiasm	18. positive
19. earnest	19. euphoria	19. quiet

20. engrossed	20. excitement	20. reassured
21. enthrallment	21. exhilaration	21. receptive
22. enthusiastic	22. festive	22. relaxed
23. fascinated	23. fortunate	23. relief
24. fondness	24. free	24. satisfied
25. good	25. frisky	25. secure
26. impulsive	26. gaiety	26. serene
27. infatuation	27. gladness	27. strong
28. inquisitive	28. glee	28. sure
29. inspired	29. great	29. thankful
30. intent	30. happiness	30. wonderful
31. interested	31. hopeful	
32. intrigued	32. impulsive	
33. kind	33. jolliness	
34. liking	34. joviality	
35. longing	35. joyous	
36. loved	36. jubilant	
37. loving	37. jubilation	
38. passionate	38. liberated	
39. pity	39. merry	
40. rapture	40. optimistic	
41. re-enforced	41. overjoyed	
42. sensitive	42. playful	
43. sentimentality	43. pleased	
44. sympathetic	44. pride	
45. tenacious	45. satisfaction	
46. tenderness	46. spirited	
47. touched	47. surprise	
48. understanding	48. thrill	
49. understood	49. triumph	
50. unique	50. zest	
51. warm		
52. zeal		

Table XXV

The Three Categories of Warning Emotions

By now, you know there are two types of human emotions. We call them "emotions of pleasure," and "emotions of warning." Notice I did not call them "positive" and "negative" emotions. Emotions are neither positive nor negative. They are neutral indicators of the state of our being. Our emotions will either indicate different types of pleasure we are experiencing or warn us that something is happening to us that needs immediate or ongoing attention. Although the emotions themselves are not positive or negative, their effects on our life are definitely positive or negative.

Just like there are three categories of pleasure emotions, there are also three categories of emotions of warning. These warning emotion categories are the exact opposites of the three categories of pleasure.

Emotions of Pleasure and Warning

Love	Joy	Peace
Anger	Sadness	Fear

Table XXVI

Just like the emotions of pleasure, all emotions of warning will fit into one of these three categories. Here is a list of these emotions to demonstrate what I mean.

Emotions of Warning

Anger	Sadness	Fear
1. abominable	1. aching	1. afflicted
2. aggravation	2. agony	2. afraid
3. aggressive	3. bored	3. alarm
4. agitation	4. defeat	4. alienation
5. annoyance	5. dejected	5. alone
6. appalled	6. depression	6. anguish
7. bad	7. desolate	7. anxiety

8. bitterness	8. despair	8. apprehension
9. boiling	9. diminishment	9. ashamed
10. cold	10. disappointment	10. challenged
11. contempt	11. discouragement	11. closed
12. cross	12. disillusionment	12. concerned
13. deprived	13. disinterest	13. confused
14. despicable	14. dismay	14. cowardly
15. detestable	15. displeasure	15. crushed
16. disgust	16. dull	16. dejection
17. dislike	17. empty	17. desperate
18. dissatisfaction	18. fatigued	18. dismayed
19. enraged	19. gloom	19. distress
20. envy	20. glumness	20. distrust
21. exasperation	21. grief	21. domination
22. ferocity	22. heartbroken	22. doubt
23. forced	23. helpless	23. dread
24. frustration	24. hopelessness	24. embarrassment
25. fuming	25. in despair	25. fright
26. fury	26. incapable	26. guilt
27. grouchiness	27. lifeless	27. hesitant
28. grumpiness	28. loss	28. homesickness
29. hate	29. melancholy	29. horror
30. hostility	30. misery	30. humiliated
31. incensed	31. mournful	31. hurt
32. indifferent	32. neutral	32. hysteria
33. indignant	33. nonchalant	33. in a stew
34. inflamed	34. pathetic	34. indecisive
35. infuriated	35. rejected	35. inferior
36. insensitive	36. sorrow	36. injured
37. insulting	37. sulky	37. insecurity
38. irritation	38. tearful	38. insult
39. jealousy	39. unhappiness	39. isolation
40. loathing	40. useless	40. loneliness
41. miserable	41. woeful	41. lost

42. offended
43. offensive
44. outrage
45. provocative
46. provoked
47. rage
48. rebellious
49. repugnant
50. resentment
51. revulsion
52. scorn
53. spite
54. stupefied
55. terrible
56. unpleasant
57. upset
58. vengefulness
59. worked up
60. wrath
61. wronged

42. menaced
43. menacing
44. misgiving
45. mortification
46. neglection
47. nervousness
48. pain
49. panic
50. paralyzed
51. perplexed
52. pessimistic
53. powerless
54. preoccupied
55. quaking
56. regret
57. remorse
58. reserved
59. restless
60. scared
61. shaky
62. shame
63. shock
64. shy
65. skeptical
66. snoopy
67. suffering
68. suspicious
69. tenseness
70. terrified
71. threatened
72. timid
73. tormented
74. tortured
75. tragic

		76. unbelieving
		77. uncertain
		78. uneasiness
		79. unsure
		80. victimized
		81. vulnerable
		82. wary
		83. worried

Table XXVII

What Should We Think About?

After our emotions of warning have served us and we have processed the event file in which they are registering, don't keep thinking about them. God never intended for the emotions of warning to continue to register! Long-term exposure to the chemicals our body releases when the emotions of warning are registering has been proven to cause diseases like cancer and diabetes. If you are a worrier, you may get sick more often, because stress these emotions put on your body can compromise your immune system. If you are continually angry or bitter, these emotions can wear your body down and potentially shorten your life.

What we think about most of the time will determine how we feel emotionally. This is because, whenever we open an event file for review, the emotional indicators are reset to where they were when that event took place.

God has provided emotions of pleasure so we can enjoy the life He has given to us. In our busy day-to-day world, sensitivity to emotions, often times, becomes dull, and we miss the very things God brings into our lives to provide us with pleasure. That is why the saying was coined, "You've got to take time to smell the roses." The importance of smelling a rose has very little to do with the flower's odor but much to do with the emotional indicators like peace, joy, and love that the rose's smell triggers.

When we sniff a rose, our brain immediately searches our memory banks for that scent or one close to it. When it finds pleasant scents in our memory banks, it opens those files for additional information about that smell. When our mind opens these files that contain pleasant scents, our brain resets our emotional indicators to what they were set at during those remembered experiences. Therefore, the stimulus of sweet smells helps to reset our emotional indicators to a healthy setting. This releases us from the effects of continual exposure to the emotions of warning. Of course, the more we spend time smelling roses, the more pleasant memories we are creating for future review.

It also provides a perfect backdrop for the emotions of warning to function best. If the normal setting of our indicators is for the emotions of pleasure to always register, then when the emotions of warning begin to register, the sharp contrast serves as an early warning system. If our emotions of warning are always registering, there is no contrast and, consequently, no early warning.

God intends for us to experience these pleasurable emotions on a daily, hourly, and moment-by-moment basis. This seems to be very necessary for obtaining and maintaining our overall health on all levels of our being—spirit, soul, and body. As a matter of fact, continually experiencing these pleasurable emotions is so important to our complete overall health that God commanded us to constantly and consciously recall memories that trigger these pleasurable emotional indicator settings.

> *Finally, brethren, whatsoever things are true, whatsoever things are honest, whatsoever things are just, whatsoever things are pure, whatsoever things are lovely, whatsoever things are of good report; if there be any virtue, and if there be any praise, think on these things. Philippians 4:8 KJV*

Let's look briefly at this list of pleasurable memory files that we are commanded to think about all the time.

Things that are true: We have already talked about how everything untrue is of the devil. Even half-truths are half lies. Also, unsubstantiated reports may or may not be true, so don't spend a lot of time thinking about what might be true. The ultimate truth we should be thinking about all the time is the Word of Truth.

> *Blessed is the man Who walks not in the counsel of the ungodly, Nor stands in the path of sinners, Nor sits in the seat of the scornful; But his delight is in the law (Word) of the Lord,) And in His law he meditates day and night. Psalm 1:1–2 NKJV*

Things that are honest: Truth can apply to one event file at a time, but someone who is honest is truthful all the time, faithfully. This means he or she has taken on Christ's character in that area of his or her life, which is so refreshing to be around and think about. The world has done away with absolutes by introducing situational ethics into our public school classrooms. That teaches our children there are some situations where it is right to be dishonest. The Bible definitely does *not* teach that!

Things that are just: This is one of God's universal laws that spans both the natural and the spiritual realms:

> *Do not be deceived, God is not mocked; for whatever a man sows, that he will also reap. Galatians 6:7 NKJV*

We can rest assured that our God is a just God and that there will be no injustice in His kingdom. Even if his timing of justice does not match ours, God will hold every person responsible for his or her actions.

Things that are pure: That which is pure has not been tainted by something foreign to it. Pureness is a thing of true beauty.

Things that are lovely: Something "lovely" is also something beautiful. It is so wonderful that you love it. It is the ultimate feel-good memory.

Things that are of good report: To the flesh, bad reports are what we are drawn to. That's why every news show spends 99 percent of its time on bad reports. A dear friend of mine, Dr. Robert Bean, whose doctorate is in psychology, explained to me the reason why our natural man is drawn to negative reports. "We are fixers," he said. "We want to be quick to recognize a problem so we can fix it before it becomes a bigger problem." Although we never can fix anything we hear on the news, we justify feeding our mind on it as education for our future. We store the conclusions of those people in an event file, in case we ever find ourselves in a similar situation.

These are not the things God wants us to continuously think about. That keeps our warning indicators always registering. By the way, for our emotions of warning to be effective, God made it so they will always register stronger than the emotions of pleasure.

Things of virtue and praise: I believe these are two categories of memory files in which the first six type of files fit. Let me explain what I mean. According to Merriam-Webster's online dictionary, the only synonym listed for "virtuous" is the word "righteous." The first three types of memory files in Philippians 4:8 all fit into the category of virtuous or righteous experiences—true, honest, and just. The next three types of memory files fit into the category of "praiseworthy" memories—pure, lovely, and of good report. We could also call these "beautiful memories."

Two Types of Pleasant Memories

	Virtuous memories	Praiseworthy memories
	Righteous Memories	Beautiful Memories
Philippians 4:8	True	Pure
	Honest	Lovely
	Just	Good Report

Table XXVIII

Because of all the untruth, dishonesty, and injustice we experience in our lives as a result of sin in the world, it is refreshing to meditate on every experience we have had, or others have had, in which virtuousness or righteousness prevailed. This also helps keep us from getting bitter over the nonvirtuous memories in our past.

Likewise, because of the influence of sin in the world, we all have impure and unlovely experiences, as well as bad reports to deal with. No one in the world will ever escape these types of experiences, but by being commanded to think on virtuous and praiseworthy memories, we are also being commanded to *not* think about the nonvirtuous and nonpraiseworthy memories. The main reason for this is to protect all three parts of our entire being from the destructive side effects associated with continual exposure to the strong emotions of warning and their corresponding memories.

Since the world fell into sin's influence through Adam, God's redemption plan for mankind also involved bringing the kingdom of God back to the realm of mankind through Jesus. The reason Jesus brought the kingdom of God to us on earth is so we could continually experience the pleasurable emotions in both of these categories (virtue and praise). As a matter of fact, both of these pleasurable emotional categories are mentioned in this scripture as foundational tenants of the kingdom of God.

> *For the kingdom of God is not meat and drink; but righteousness, and peace, and joy in the Holy Ghost. Romans 14:17 KJV*

Notice the two categories once again. Keep in mind that peace and joy are two emotional indicators that epitomize the beautiful and praiseworthy categories of pleasurable emotions.

Pleasant Memories/The Kingdom Chart #1

	Virtuous memories	Praiseworthy memories
	Righteous Memories	Beautiful Memories
Philippians 4:8	True	Pure
	Honest	Lovely
	Just	Good Report
Romans 14:17	Righteousness	Peace and Joy

Table XXIX

These two categories of pleasurable emotions are noted throughout the scripture, both in the Old and New Testaments. Here is a New Testament reference to an Old Testament event, which talks about these two categories of pleasurable memories and their origins being found in the Old Testament Theophany named Melchisedec.

> *For this Melchisedec, king of Salem, priest of the most high God, who met Abraham returning from the slaughter of the kings, and blessed him; To whom also Abraham gave a tenth part of all; first being by interpretation King of righteousness, and after that also King of Salem, which is, King of peace; Without father, without mother, without descent, having neither beginning of days, nor end of life; but made like unto the Son of God; abideth a priest continually. Hebrews 7:1–3 KJV*

We see that this Old Testament manifestation of God himself to Abraham is called "King" over both of these two categories of pleasure that describe the "kingdom of God."

Pleasant Memories/The Kingdom Chart #2

	Virtuous memories	Praiseworthy memories
	Righteous Memories	Beautiful Memories
Philippians 4:8	True	Pure
	Honest	Lovely
	Just	Good Report
Romans 14:17	Righteousness	Peace and Joy
Hebrews 7:1–3	King of righteousness	King of peace

Table XXX

If we experience one of these categories of pleasurable memories, it helps us to experience the other category as well.

> *And the fruit of righteousness is sown in peace of them that make peace. James 3:18 KJV*

Pleasant Memories/The Kingdom Chart #3

	Virtuous memories	Praiseworthy memories
	Righteous Memories	Beautiful Memories
Philippians 4:8	True	Pure
	Honest	Lovely
	Just	Good Report
Romans 14:17	Righteousness	Peace and Joy
Hebrews 7:1–3	King of righteousness	King of peace
James 3:18	Righteousness	Peace

Table XXXI

Let me share just one more scripture with you concerning these two biblical categories of pleasurable memories. Notice we will return to the use of the word "praise," indicating the praiseworthy memories, instead of simply listing the emotions.

For as the earth bringeth forth her bud, and as the garden causeth the things that are sown in it to spring forth; so the Lord GOD will cause righteousness and praise to spring forth before all the nations. Isaiah 61:11 KJV

Pleasant Memories/The Kingdom Chart #4

	Virtuous memories	Praiseworthy memories
	Righteous Memories	Beautiful Memories
Philippians 4:8	True	Pure
	Honest	Lovely
	Just	Good Report
Romans 14:17	Righteousness	Peace and Joy
Hebrews 7:1–3	King of righteousness	King of peace
James 3:18	Righteousness	Peace
Isaiah 61:11	Righteousness	Praise

Table XXXII

The Function of the Mind in Worship

We first looked at Psalms 100 in Chapter Six of *Biblical Worship*. We reviewed it again in this book in Chapter One under the subtitle "What Does Creation Have to Do with Worship?" Now we want to dive in a little deeper into its truths, because it outlines for us the way we are to use the three cognitive functions of our mind as we worship the Lord. Some of these concepts we introduced before; however, you should be able to understand them more completely now. It's a short Psalm, so let's read the whole thing again.

Make a joyful noise unto the Lord, all ye lands. Serve the Lord with gladness: come before his presence with singing. Know ye that the Lord he is God: it is he that hath made us, and not we ourselves; we are his people, and the sheep of his pasture. Enter into his gates with thanksgiving, and into his courts with praise: be thankful unto him,

and bless his name. For the Lord is good; his mercy is
everlasting; and his truth endureth to all generations.
Psalm 100:1–5 KJV

Again, this is the most important chapter in the Bible concerning praise and worship. We will speak about it often in our studies on worship. Let's do a quick study of all five verses, and in it we will discover the function of the mind in worship.

The first phrase of this Psalm is translated "Make a joyful shout to the Lord" in the New King James version. Since we have learned that shouting is a biblical expression of worship and since this noisy shout is directed to the Lord, we know that the subject of this Psalm is "Praising God."

The second phrase of this Psalm, "Serve the Lord with gladness," reminds us that our service to God is our worship of God. It also tells us that our service to God must be done with an attitude of gladness, not obligation.

The next phrase, "come before his presence with singing," first reminds us that one of the purposes of our worship is to experience God's presence. The Lord has told us that the quickest and most effective way to experience His presence here on earth is to praise and worship Him.

> *But thou art holy, O thou that inhabitest the praises of*
> *Israel. Psalms 22:3 KJV*

Remember that the goal of our worship is to experience God's presence and that will be the result. To experience the presence of God means we will get to know God more each time we worship Him.

The memory files of when we experienced God's presence contain the emotional indicator settings prompted by His presence. However, not every encounter with God's presence will produce the exact same emotional settings. Therefore, you cannot use the emotional indicators as verification of God's presence. Our spirit is the part of our being that detects God's presence and anointing, not our emotions.

> *The Spirit itself beareth witness with our spirit, that we*
> *are the children of God: Romans 8:16 KJV*

If we equate God's presence with particular emotional indicator settings, it is easy to seek after that overall feeling in our worship, rather than the One whose presence gives us the feelings. Because of the widespread misunderstanding of what causes our emotional feelings to register, I have seen many people trying to recreate a desired emotional setting that they associate with God's presence by attempting to recreate the prior physical actions of worship or previous emotional worship experiences, thinking certain postures or expressions of worship usher God in. When in truth, it was their obedience to the Spirit of God's initiation of worship to be expressed in the ways He desired at that moment that pleased God and brought His presence to them at that time.

When we worship, we should never seek to recreate the same emotional indicator settings as we experienced before in worship. We should only seek Jesus' face and presence and allow Him to give us unique and different emotional feelings with every touch of His presence. We don't seek a feeling—we seek His person.

The second part of the phrase in Psalms 100:2 is a commandment for all of us to worship the Lord by singing. It is a lie from the devil to think some of us can sing, and some of us cannot sing. To believe that concept is to believe that God is mean and cruel. God is not up in heaven looking down at you saying, "Hey angels, come here! I commanded them all to sing, but I made this one so he can't sing. Listen, it will be funny!"

God would never command you to do something if He had not first equipped you to be able to do it. There is no such thing as tone deafness—only inexperience in matching pitches! My music degree is in voice, and I have been teaching voice since 1976. I have never failed at teaching any of the hundreds of students how to match pitches, because God has equipped every person with the ability to hear whether he or she is singing the correct note. The number one reason why people do not think they can sing is fear.

Singing is the most powerful expression of corporate worship God has given us. That's why Satan hates singing so much and tries so hard to keep you from singing. Singing is to corporate worship what prayer is to individual worship. Prayer is the most powerful expression of worship that God has given to us as individuals. We will discuss the reasons why singing is so powerful in the next book of this series, *Corporate Worship*.

Let's get back to our discussion of Psalms 100. Verses three and four contain the insights we need to explain the function of the mind in worship. Let's read it again.

> *Know ye that the Lord he is God: it is he that hath made us, and not we ourselves; we are his people, and the sheep of his pasture. Enter into his gates with thanksgiving, and into his courts with praise: Psalm 100:3–4 KJV*

Our mental processes when we worship must begin from the knowledge of whom we are worshipping. Every time you worship, start with the knowledge of who God is. In this case, David chose to remember God as our creator as his focal mental starting point in this time of worship. You can also choose to start other times of worship remembering that God is your Savior or healer or provider, etc. Be led of the Spirit as to which knowledge of God He wants you to begin with.

In our example, the knowledge of God being the one who made us gave place quickly to the deductive reasoning or thoughts that, if God made us, we couldn't have made ourselves. From that point, our meditative reasoning concludes that, if God made us, we belong to him. We are His people—He owns us. We are not our own!

At this point of the mental processes in our worship, we slip into imaginations. David's imaginations gravitated to the subject he knew the most about at that time of his life, sheep.

We are His people just like sheep belong to a shepherd. We are His sheep, and He makes sure we are fed in His pasture. When it's time to sleep at night, He brings us through His gate—and we are so thankful for that—and he protects us all night long inside His courtyard, for which we all sing praise to Him.

> *be thankful unto him, and bless his name. For the Lord is good; his mercy is everlasting; and his truth endureth to all generations. Psalm 100:4b–5 KJV*

The second part of verse four speaks to our attitude and heart motivation when we worship. Giving thanks is an action. Being thankful is an attitude. It is impossible to give thanks without a thankful attitude. Being thankful is where all worship starts. All worship is birthed out of thankfulness. That's why it is the gate. To "bless His Name" keeps our focus on blessing Him, not ourselves.

Finally, verse five speaks of new revelation knowledge of who God is. By spending time in His presence, God will always reveal more of Himself to the worshiper. In this worship experience, God revealed new revelation knowledge to David about who He is in light of His goodness, mercy, and truth. When we look at the next Psalm, Psalm 101, we see David starting from this new knowledge about God's mercy.

When we worship, all three functions of our conscience mind should be involved. At no time in worship should our mind be disengaged or focused on anything other than the Lord. Even split seconds of carnal thoughts cause our worship to be short circuited and disqualified, like these examples.

"Halleluiah, praise the Lord! Did I lock the house when we left this morning?"

"You are awesome! You are holy! Where should we go for lunch after church today?"

Let it never be said of us what Jesus said in this scripture!

> 'These people draw near to Me with their mouth, And honor Me with their lips, But their heart (mind and emotions are) is far from Me. Matthew 15:8 NKJV

Notice this progression in our worship. Thanksgiving, or an attitude of thankfulness, is the first step toward God's presence. Praise is what the Lord inhabits.[72] When we worship and praise Him with no short

Steps to Know God

---

[72] Ps. 22:3.

circuits, we experience His presence. When we are in God's presence, He always reveals Himself more to us, so we get to know Him better.

Reading Our Emotions

If our emotions would register one at a time, then we would not struggle to figure out exactly what we are feeling in any given experience. However, all our emotional indicators register at the same time, making it difficult for us to isolate each individual emotion and determine what we are feeling and how much we are feeling it.

Remember, each emotion within us is its own meter or indicator, and it contributes to the overall report of the category meter. Each indicator registers independently of the other meters, yet each emotion can be influenced by the other emotions, depending on how high the other emotions register.

As we discuss our emotions, we must keep in mind that they are part of our soul, which is still in the process of being redeemed or delivered, as long as we are on this earth.

When someone asks you how you feel, he or she is usually asking you how you feel physically. Since most people think of themselves primarily as a physical being, most people hear and answer that question on the physical level. However, having spent well over forty years in ministry, with some postgraduate studies in counseling, and having spent hundreds of hours counseling all types of cases, I think of that question as being asked on the emotional level just as much as on the physical level. As a matter of fact, the question a counselor is trained to ask of a counselee on a regular basis is, "And, how do you *feel* about that?" This is to help the client get in touch with his or her emotions.

There are many reasons why someone would be unable to read his or her emotional indicators. One possibility would be traumatic experiences where feelings have been suppressed. Some traumatized people do not think they have the right to have certain feelings. In that case, the therapist would endeavor to reassure the counseling client that it is OK to have emotional feelings. Emotions only become wrong when we act out of them in destructive or hurtful ways. There are hundreds of other reasons why people are hindered from properly recognizing and reading the emotions they experience in day-to-day life.

Humans not only need to be in touch with their emotions (which means to identify and read them correctly) but also to know how to process the emotions properly. Without these two factors being developed in our lives, we will become emotionally unhealthy individuals.

By processing the emotional indicators associated with any life experience, we will determine possible responses to that experience. However, before acting out any of these possible responses, two more determinations should always be made. We need to examine these possible actions according to Godly principles of truth and God's will or leading for that moment.

Multiple, simultaneous meter settings sometimes make it difficult for us to put into words how we are feeling at the time of an experience, especially if several very different emotional meters are registering high at the same time.

Emotions of Warning figure one

If one emotion is registering higher than the rest of the emotions, we will usually conclude and store the memory of how we feel about an experience under the name of the predominant feeling. For instance, if both our anger indicator and fear indicator are registering, yet the anger registers higher than the fear, we will tend to describe the way we feel as angry, not fearful. The added fear to our anger could actually have a positive result by instilling caution to keep us from acting out of our anger.

Here are the indicators registering both of these emotions as well. Even though we are just as mad as

Emotions of Warning figure two

the first scenario, the absence of fear could make us more dangerous, because we may have no caution about acting out of our anger.

As I have said, it is easiest to know how we feel about any given experience in life when one emotion is predominantly responding over all the rest. However, that very seldom happens. Usually we will experience a mixture of emotions all at the same time. This is why we many times say, "I'm not sure how I feel right now."

When many different emotions are registering at the same time, it takes a while to sort out which emotions are registering and how much they are registering. Since it takes time to process the emotional settings associated with any given multiemotional experience, we usually must do so by reopening the memory file of that experience several times and reading those emotional settings until we understand that experience's settings of the emotional indicators, along with all the other pertinent data associated with that experience's memory.

When we reopen a memory file of an experience, we will experience every emotion the same as we did at the time of the experience we are remembering. These emotional indicator levels will always occur when we think about that event, until we process the file. Sometimes the processing of memory files can happen during our sleep, whereas other memory files require our conscience mind to be involved.

If an experience is acutely emotionally painful, we may stay away from reopening that file, which means—nine times out of ten—we never will understand exactly how we feel or felt about that experience, because it is too painful to think about. The flip side of that "coin" is that we become consumed with that unresolved, unprocessed memory and think about it all the time, because it bothers us that we have not yet been able to unravel the way we feel about that experience, the reasons we feel that way, and what we should do about it.

This second scenario is very dangerous. Keeping the emotions of warning registering high for long periods of time has a very unhealthy effect on both our soul and body. These emotions cause chemicals that are meant to help us in the short term but that can cause cancer and other disease in the long term to be released into the body.

By the way, generally, women process—or read—their emotions best by talking about them, while men tend to process their emotions by thinking about them. This can be a source of frustration in relationships between men and women, if you do not know this.

Please keep in mind that whenever the memory file of an experience is opened, our brain resets the emotional indicators to the way they were at that experience. Therefore, when we remember an experience, we feel the same way we did when that memory was made. In other words, the memories of the mind carry with them the settings of our emotional indicators.

> *This I recall to my mind, therefore have I hope.*
> *Lamentations 3:21 KJV*

By recalling this particular memory, Jeremiah's hope indicator began to register. Remembering what God has done for us in the past will give us hope for the future.

Of course, this also happens with the data from the five senses. Have you ever remembered an experience in your life where you could smell what you smelled then or taste what you tasted then, even though it was just a memory? I can remember wearing a wool sweater my mother bought me, thinking it would keep me warm. Every time I think about that, I immediately start to scratch myself, even though I am not actually wearing wool. Memories have a very powerful effect on both our soul and body.

To endure the necessary procedure of processing our emotions regarding an experience, without having the acuteness of the severity of the high registering emotional indicators, simply tell your brain, "This is just the memory of this experience, not the actual experience itself." Instruct your brain to only leave the emotional indicator settings at the levels they were during the remembered experience long enough for you to take a screenshot of them; then instruct your mind to dial them all back several points—all an equal amount—while you are processing this memory file. This takes the edge off what you were feeling, which lets you process the file more efficiently. Your brain is a phenomenal organ, and it can do this, as long as you remind it that you are not in the experience at that moment but are only remembering the experience.

Processing emotions is easiest for individuals who are emotionally healthy. However, even for a well-balanced person, it is still not easy to do when our emotional indicator settings are nowhere like any other memory of indicator settings we have had before.

Part of the processing of our memories is determining how we feel at the time of any memory in two ways. First, for every experience we have, we remember the settings of every individual emotional indicator. Then we also remember the overall feeling that resulted from that particular combination of emotional meter settings. Every experience, or memory, will feel slightly different overall from most other memories, because of the slightly different combination of emotional indicator settings that are possible. The number of different combinations of emotional indicator settings is almost limitless. That's why we can be senior citizens and still be able to have an experience where we can say we have never emotionally felt quite that way before.

For those who are functioning from emotional weakness or sickness, it can seem almost impossible to sort out the emotional indicators without help. It is important that we all learn how to identify every one of our emotions and how to read the level our emotions are registering so that we can use the emotions as God intended for them to be used—to indicate to us the state of our inner being.

The healthy way to use emotions of warning is to see them as indications that something is not right concerning our being or life. This warning should then trigger a self-examination to determine where the problem originates and what we should do about the problem. Emotions of warning should never be treated as a license to react or respond improperly. They only should tip us off that something is not quite right, and it needs to be addressed in some way.

There are no pat answers or formulas to follow when these emotions of warning start registering. In other words, when you sense anger, you should not automatically share that anger with the object of the emotion, as some suggest. We must take two actions immediately when we detect an emotional indication of warning. First, we must examine the situation according to the principles of the Word of Truth. Second, we must immediately start to pray to God for wisdom in every situation. The truth is that only God knows the best course of action. Last time you experienced anger, it might have been right to share it. But this time it may be wrong to share your feelings right away. Only God knows what is happening with every person involved and what would be best for each of them at this given time. The important thing for you is to recognize that you have anger registering in your being. Do not ignore this emotional indicator, and do not act out of how you feel until God gives you instructions.

When any emotional indicator of warning begins to register, wait for God's direction in that situation before taking any action. This means you may end up doing nothing for a while until you hear from God about the situation. If God does not give instructions right away, store the memory file, then return to the Philippians 4:8 principle, keeping only the closed file at the front of your memory as a reminder to continue to seek God for wisdom for the situation.

An Exercise in Reading Your Indicators

Study the graphic on the next page. Carefully look at where these indicators are registering, then determine how this person is feeling right now. You may even want to do some speculation as to what might have brought on how this person is feeling at this time.

As an exercise in processing emotions, pretend you are this person and journal how you are feeling right now. To express yourself on this emotional level, tell what you have experienced to get to this emotional state. The experiences you share can come from one of three places.

> ➢ They can be totally imaginary or fictional.
> ➢ They can be experiences you have observed others around you go through.
> ➢ They can be your own past experiences.

For this exercise, role-play. This means that, even if you are making up the whole story, tell it in first-person point of view as though you are the person who has experienced these things. What you share, however, *cannot* come from other people's fiction or imaginations, such as in the case of a book, a movie, or a television show.

Emotions

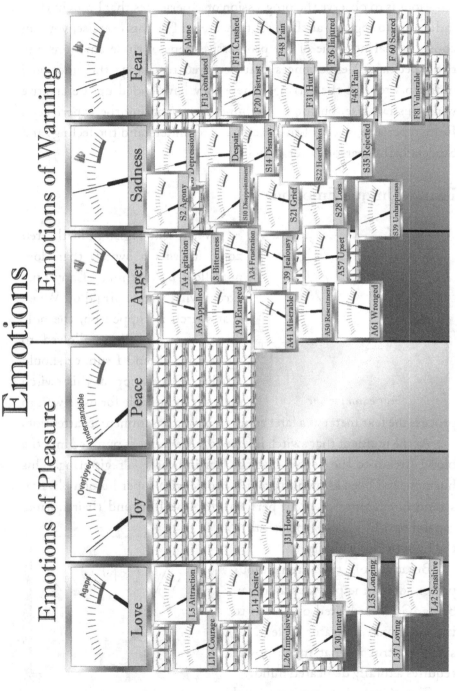

Example Emotional Experience

One of the ways people learn to recognize and read their own emotions is to observe the progression of experiences that brought their indicators to register at the level they are at. For this exercise, you can consider sharing some of the progressive steps of these emotions and the (speculated) experiences that occurred to change the emotional indicators toward the settings where they have ended up. Be creative with this exercise, but don't get hung up on sharing the experiences. Remember, the object of this exercise is to understand the feelings and especially this person's overall feelings.

Fear, a Unique Emotion

Fear example one

When fear registers in the red zone, it trips a switch that does not allow us to think of anything except what we are afraid of. When that switch is flipped on, the only question our brain is allowed to answer is, "Should I run, or should I fight?" Once tripped, this switch makes it impossible for us to wait to process the fear meter at a later time. It commands immediate attention.

At the moment that switch is flipped, adrenaline is pumped into the blood stream to the degree that the fear indicator is registering. This hormone has been known to provide people with super-human physical strength, enabling them to perform feats well beyond their normal capabilities. In science, this is called the fight-or-flight ability.

Because of the tremendous power adrenaline provides a human being, God hardwired our brain to the emotional indicator of fear. To safely control it, that much power requires a totally dedicated mind.

Therefore, when our emotional

Fear example two

indicator of fear reaches the red zone, it flips that switch that turns off all other conscious functions of the mind, allowing the mind to only focus on what is causing the fear. The only way to allow other conscience functions of the mind to happen simultaneously with the emotional indicator of fear is to get the indicator to register below the red zone so that it turns off that override switch.

Driving through Banff National Park in Canada one day, my family and I came across some bear cubs by the side of the road, and a man outside his car, inching toward them with a very expensive camera, trying to get a picture of them. Suddenly, Mama Bear thought this guy was too close to her babies and came out of the tree line on her back legs. She then dropped to all fours and charged the man. I was sure we were about to watch him die, but he dropped his camera and barely made it inside his car before the bear got there. It was close! He never went back for his camera but sped away as fast as he could. Fear served him well that day. It kept him alive.

Anger and Sadness

Just like fear, anger and sadness also have override switches. When tripped, these switches turn off the conscience functions of the mind. In other words, it is impossible to reason when the emotions of warning are in the red zone. That means it is impossible to process any current event file until these three meters have been dialed back.

Never make any decisions or take any actions when anger and sadness are in the red zone. If you do, I guarantee it will be an unreasonable choice, because you have *no* ability to think or reason at that time. This is different from the fear indicator, which commands an immediate decision and action.

What do you do if you find yourself with anger registering in the red zone? First, immediately remove yourself from the situation! You *must* get to a place where you are alone! Second, pray this prayer out loud. "Lord Jesus, help me with my anger! I repent for letting my anger get out of control! I am sorry, Lord! Please forgive me? Now anger, I command you in the name of Jesus to dial back to '1.' You have no right in my life to be out of control. Jesus is Lord of my life and that includes you, too, anger!"

Third, take five to ten slow, deep breaths. As you are breathing deeply, change your thoughts to comply with the Philippians 4:8 commandment. If you have trouble thinking of something virtuous or praiseworthy right away, think these thoughts as you breathe: "Out with the anger, in with the love."

Fourth, spend time reading the psalms out loud or worshipping the Lord until your emotions of pleasure override and shut down your emotions of warning. Remember, it is possible to be angry and not sin. What makes anger sin is when your override switch gets flipped and you lose self-control.

What do you do if you find yourself with sadness registering in the red zone? First, *never* let yourself be alone. You are a sitting duck for the enemy to attack you when you are alone. Get around Christians, not carnal people. The last thing you need at that time is worldly wisdom, which leads to death. If no one is available to meet with you, call someone! If you don't know anyone to call, call the 700 Club or one of the many prayer lines available to you. *Do not* think you should be able to be strong and get through this on your own. Red zone sadness has turned off your conscience mind, which means you have no ability to reason at that moment.

Second, pray this prayer out loud. Ask someone to agree with you as you pray. "Lord Jesus, help me with my sadness and depression! I repent for letting my depression get out of control! I am sorry, Lord! Please forgive me? Now depression, I command you in the name of Jesus to dial back to '1.' You have no right in my life to be out of control. Jesus is Lord of my life and that includes you, too, sadness and depression! Now I command my soul to be joyful! I am created in the likeness and image of God for the purpose of glorifying Jesus! Therefore, I will fulfill my purpose joyfully, for the joy of the Lord is my strength!"

Third, begin to worship the Lord with all your strength, no matter what you feel like. Loudly sing a worship song you know! If one doesn't come to mind, open your Bible to any Psalm and read it out loud until your emotions of pleasure override and shut down your emotions of warning.

A Lesson in Processing a Current Event File

The Christian music group New Song wrote and released a story song called *The Christmas Shoes*[73] in 2000, which is still getting radio air play in select markets around the country at Christmas time. It is a fictional example of how further investigation can immediately change our emotional indicator settings. This song was well-crafted to tell the story of a man who found himself in another long checkout line on Christmas Eve behind a young boy whose only purchase was a pair of women's shoes. After a long wait, it was finally the young boy's turn at the checkout register, so he counted his pennies, nickels, and dimes, which seemed to take forever to the man in line behind him, only to come up very short of the purchase price of the shoes.

The song presupposes that all of us have found ourselves in a similar situation and that, upon this reminder, we will search our memory banks for that, or those, incidents for more information. Once we find our own files like this story, where we have been in a hurry and had to wait on someone else, we immediately know some of the thoughts that were racing through that man's head as he stood there waiting, having his frustration meter registering close to the red zone. His anger meter was not far behind his frustration, as his thoughts raced from one memory file to another and then just as quickly back to the current situation and all that he still had to do before the stores close early that Christmas Eve.

Then this man finds out what he did not know. Without intentionally seeking out more information about this situation, the young boy volunteers the data that changed this man's emotional indicators in a moment's time. The chorus of this great song begins like this. "Sir, I want to buy these shoes for my momma, please. It's Christmas Eve, and these shoes are just her size." It goes on to reveal the boy's frustration that the

---

[73] Carswell, Eddie and Leonard Ahlstrom, *The Christmas Shoes*, Sony/ATV Songs LLC and WB Music Corp./Jerry's Haven Music, 2000, compact disc.

purchase was taking a while, because his dad had told him there was not much time left for his momma to live. Then the chorus concludes, "She's been sick for quite a while. I know these shoes will make her smile. I want her to look beautiful if momma meets Jesus tonight."[74]

This small amount of information is enough for the man's frustration and anger meters to cease registering and for the sympathy and empathy meters to peg past the red zone. The musical bridge of this song reveals the result of this man immediately processing all the data he had received concerning this incident. It continues, "So I laid the money down. I just had to help him out!" This action reveals the conclusions this man reached as he immediately processed all the data of that experience. By this action, we know how he feels, what he thinks, and obviously what he did about this experience.

One more thing happens as a result of this experience. In all of the memory files that were opened while the man was processing this experience, a link was placed to this current event file to remind the man not to let his frustration and anger meters register so high in any future situations like this one. Also, more tolerant possibilities for reasons and motives surrounding those memories are immediately written into those open files, and the emotional indicator settings for those more tolerant possibilities were experienced and recorded for any future reference to all those files. The conclusion in the song's bridge says, "I know God sent that little boy to remind me what Christmas is all about."

In other words, the result of this one correctly processed experience changed the way this man now looks at all of his past similar experiences and how he will look at all future similar experiences. The telling of this story to us also has the same effect on all our similar files.

Emotions of Pleasure as Emotions of Warning

All emotions can be used as emotions of warning in any given circumstance, even love. What determines if an emotion will be a

---

[74] Carswell, Eddie and Leonard Ahlstrom, *The Christmas Shoes*, Sony/ATV Songs LLC and WB Music Corp./Jerry's Haven Music, 2000, compact disc.

warning to us or an indication of true Godly pleasure is the principles of Godly truth being applied to our life.

For instance, a Christian man, who has made Jesus Lord of his life and who is married, may begin to experience a registering of the emotional indicator love for another woman other than his wife. This should be a real big warning to that man to examine his emotions according to the Godly truth of his marriage vows to his wife before God. In this instance, this man's soul may cause the love and joy meters to register very high when he thinks about the other woman. However, this man's spirit will register high readings of fear and caution.

The combination of these emotional indicators of love and fear should produce the warning necessary for self-examination according to the Word of Truth. The Word of Truth will establish righteousness in this situation, if the man seeks and accepts it without prejudice. Back in the 1980s, Christian music artist Don Francisco wrote a song that stated, "Love is not a feeling; it's an act of your will."[75] A marriage vow is a covenant, which is binding. It has nothing to do with the way you feel. Feelings follow commitment or actions. Actions should *never* follow feelings!

Another example of emotions of pleasure acting as emotions of warning is if someone has high indications of happiness when he or she sees someone else hurt. Although joy and happiness may be the only meters registering at that time, by examining the experience file with the Word of Truth, we quickly know that joy is not an appropriate emotional response. Therefore, the warning lights should start to flash, indicating something is wrong that needs to be fixed.

The Will Is the Internal Switch

Our emotions can either indicate the state of our soul or the state of our Spirit. This question then arises: How do we know when the emotional indicators are reflecting the state of our soul or our spirit?

---

[75] Francisco, Don. https://www.youtube.com/watch?v=mKbHFMADh8Y Love is not a Feeling, words and music by Don Francisco, published by Benson Music, © 1984, released on the "Holiness" album on the NewPax label

For the answer to this question, I refer you to our study of Hebrews 4:12 in this book.

> *For the word of God is quick, and powerful, and sharper than any twoedged sword, piercing even to the dividing asunder of soul and spirit, and of the joints and marrow, and is a discerner of the thoughts and intents of the heart. Hebrews 4:12 KJV*

Remember, we said that it is by spending time in the Word of God that makes it possible for us to discern the difference between what is happening with our spirit and what is happening with our soul. And we indicated that, to the degree that we have been taught by the Spirit and Word of Truth is the degree that we will discern the difference between our soul and spirit.

The Will is our switch

Our spirit and soul use the emotional indicators to indicate the state of our being. However, at no time will the indicators register data from both the soul and the spirit at the same time. The carnal mind is at enmity with the spirit,[76] therefore they cannot share the meter at the same time. By an act of our will, we can switch our meters to receive data from either our soul or our spirit. And this switch can be flipped very quickly when you learn how to do it.

What causes our soul to experience joy, especially the unredeemed part of our soul, will not be what causes our spirit to experience joy. This same thing is also true for every one of our emotional indicators, even the indicators of warning.

When our meters of pleasure and warning pick up what is happening in our spirit, they are actually picking up on what is taking place in God's heart, which is joined to our spirit. The same emotional indicators used

---

[76] Rom. 8:7–8.

to detect the presence of jealousy, anger, or fear in our soul will also tell us when God is feeling these things as well. Paul understood this very well and mentioned two of these indicators of warning in this passage of scripture.

> *Would to God ye could bear with me a little in my folly: and indeed bear with me. For I am jealous over you with godly jealousy: for I have espoused you to one husband, that I may present you as a chaste virgin to Christ. But I fear, lest by any means, as the serpent beguiled Eve through his subtlety, so your minds should be corrupted from the simplicity that is in Christ. 2 Corinthians 11:1–3 KJV*

This was not natural jealousy Paul was feeling—it was "Godly jealousy," coming from the Spirit of God within him. Likewise, his fear mentioned here was not based in natural concern for the Corinthians but in Spiritual concern over their spiritual well-being. At this time, Paul's emotional indicators were reflecting the state of his spiritual being.

Even Jesus, who we are told did not sin even once when He was in the flesh on this earth, experienced great (red zone level) anger several times in His earthly life. Jesus is God, who is incapable of sin.

> *For we have not an high priest which cannot be touched with the feeling of our infirmities; but was in all points tempted like as we are, yet without sin. Hebrews 4:15 KJV*

Here is one of the times where Jesus displayed an incredible level of anger.

> *And the Jews' passover was at hand, and Jesus went up to Jerusalem, And found in the temple those that sold oxen and sheep and doves, and the changers of money sitting: And when he had made a scourge of small cords, he drove them all out of the temple, and the sheep, and the oxen; and poured out the changers' money, and overthrew the tables; And said unto them that sold doves, Take these things hence; make not my Father's house an house of*

merchandise. And his disciples remembered that it was written, The zeal of thine house hath eaten me up. John 2:13–17 KJV

This is quite a demonstration of anger from Jesus, yet in it He still did not sin, because it was Godly anger, not carnal anger. His actions were in defense of righteousness, not the desires of the flesh. Carnal anger will almost always lead us into sin; yet it is possible to be angry even as humans and not sin.

Therefore each of you must put off falsehood and speak truthfully to his neighbor, for we are all members of one body. In your anger do not sin: Do not let the sun go down while you are still angry, and do not give the devil a foothold. Ephesians 4:25–27NIV

Every one of us will experience anger in our lives. The only way to make sure we do not sin with this anger is to process the experience file containing this anger before the day is out. Don't leave anger files to be processed another day, even if the anger is indicating the state of our spirit. Anger is a destroyer of everything that is good. When the emotional indicator anger starts registering, it is like a time bomb. It must be defused before it blows up and destroys everything it is touching. The fact is you will not be able to tell if your anger meter is registering the state of your soul or your spirit until you properly process the file, which includes allowing the file to be examined by the Word of Truth. Plus, spiritually motivated anger will be transferred to our soul if the anger is not processed right away. This will then result in sin. In other words, never go to bed with your emotions of warning still registering. Always follow the Philippians 4:8 commandment before you go to sleep.

The Dangers of Choosing Not to Worship

One of the most balanced Bible teachers I have ever known is Malcom Smith.[77] In his teaching series on the book of Romans, he explained the two different types of Godly wrath. This is a summarization of what he taught.

There are two types of wrath mentioned in the Bible. The first type is the one we are all familiar with, which the Bible calls the "day of wrath" or the "day of judgment." This day is mentioned in these two scriptures.

> *The Lord knoweth how to deliver the godly out of temptations, and to reserve the unjust unto the day of judgment to be punished: 2 Peter 2:9 KJV*

> *But after thy hardness and impenitent heart treasurest up unto thyself wrath against the day of wrath and revelation of the righteous judgment of God; Romans 2:5 KJV*

This second scripture actually mentions both types of wrath. It tells us that, while here on earth, we are gathering up wrath that will be administered on the "day of wrath" at the end of the age. So, what is the wrath we are gathering up? To understand that, start by reading these scriptures.

> *For the wrath of God is revealed from heaven against all ungodliness and unrighteousness of men, who hold the truth in unrighteousness; Because that which may be known of God is manifest in them; for God hath shewed it unto them. . . . Wherefore God also gave them up to. . . dishonor their own bodies. . . For this cause God gave them up unto vile affections. . . God gave them over to a reprobate mind Romans 1:18–19, 24, 26, 28 KJV*

The wrath that we are storing up while on Earth, Malcom Smith explained, "God gives us over to what we think we want."

---

[77] Malcom Smith, Unconditional Love Fellowships, accessed on July 16, 2017, http://unconditionallovefellowship.com/about/.

It is noteworthy to look at where this process begins. Our choice to not worship God results in an unthankful attitude. That attitude opens us up to the revealed God's wrath on this earth, which is God giving us what we think we want.

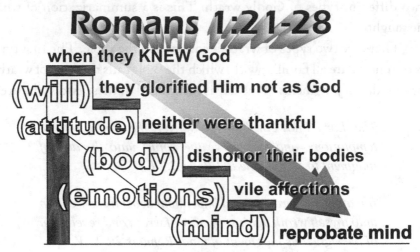

Romans 1:21-28

when they KNEW God

(will) they glorified Him not as God

(attitude) neither were thankful

(body) dishonor their bodies

(emotions) vile affections

(mind) reprobate mind

Biblical Backsliding Corrupts every part of our being, and quenches the Holy Spirit

It all depends on the will. By continually choosing to not function in the purpose for which God created and designed us, we are doomed to suffer these consequences. The wrath of God is revealed from heaven against unrighteous disobedience to our purpose. So, would you rather punish the devil for his disobedience with your worship of God or have every part of your unredeemed person become corrupted and deceived, resulting in death?

> *And if it seem evil unto you to serve the Lord, choose you this day whom ye will serve; whether the gods which your fathers served that were on the other side of the flood, or the gods of the Amorites, in whose land ye dwell: but **as for me and my house, we will serve the Lord.** Joshua 24:15 KJV, emphasis added.*

The decision teeters on your choice.

The Flesh   The Spirit

the body   our spirit

the mind   God's Spirit

the emotions   The Word

       the will

The Will Chart

Other Books by this Author

Publisher: WestBow Press
Pages: 162
Size: 6x9
ISBN: 978-1-44973-713-9

God has always had a way He wants to be worshipped. He has outlined that way for us in His written revelation—the Bible. In it, He has commanded us to worship Him with our entire being, holding nothing back. According to Jesus, this is the first and greatest commandment.

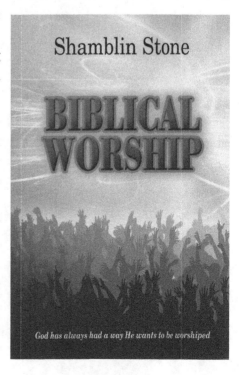

The reasons God has given us for obeying His commands to worship Him are because of who He is and because of what He does.

Worship is the biblically declared reason for mankind's existence. However, how and when we worship is just as important as the fact that we do worship. Also, what God means when He uses the biblical synonyms of the word "worship" is important to understand when we are trying to obtain a more complete picture of how God wants us to worship Him.

Biblical Worship is a book for every Christian, regardless of their preferred worship style or worship traditions. The fresh, new insights contained within its pages about what type of worship God desires from us all have the potential to shock you at times. At the very least, this book will cause you to never view worship the same way again.

A drama sketch found in John 4:3–34

A Lesson on Worship

Scripted and blocked by Shamblin Stone

Characters: Narrator, Woman of Samaria, and Jesus
Time: Bible times, the sixth hour of the day, which is noon
Setting: Jacob's well just outside Sychar, Samaria

Narrator:

After 400 years of silence, during which time there were no prophets of God who wrote their prophecies down for future generations, there came a strange prophet whose birth was declared by an angel to his father. This prophet's name was John, and his message was that of repentance. To demonstrate a repentant attitude, John demanded that people submit themselves to public water baptism. The Pharisees, who were the religious leaders of the day, hated John and his message.

A natural cousin of John's, who's birth was also foretold by angels, began his public ministry shortly after John. His message revealed Himself to the world as creator God come in the flesh to bring the Kingdom of God to mankind.

From the early years of Jesus' ministry, the Pharisees realized that Jesus made and baptized more disciples than John, which made Jesus more of a target of their anger than John. To avoid a premature confrontation with them, Jesus left Judaea and departed again into Galilee. As He traveled with His twelve chosen disciples, He told them that He must go through Samaria. Although this was highly unusual for Jews in that day, the disciples did not verbally question Jesus as to why.

There was a long-term hatred between the Jews and the Samaritans. The Samaritans were a cross-bred nation of Jews and Gentiles who were not accepted by either race. The Jews felt the Samaritans were so corrupted as human beings that they even refused to touch a Samaritan. Tradition tells us that when a Jew made a business deal with a Samaritan, the Jew would drape his cloak over his hand before shaking hands with the Samaritan to seal the deal.

Can you begin to understand the anger that had built up for generations inside the Samaritan people, based on this level of rejection openly expressed toward them? The Jews felt superior to the Samaritans and had no problem openly showing their feelings. The Samaritans took every opportunity to strike out at the Jews, out of their anger and hatred.

Our story today is about a certain Samaritan woman, one of these rejected people. Only, this woman has led such a hard life that she finds herself even rejected by the other Samaritans. To divorce and remarry in Bible times was not the same as it is today. It was the worst disgrace any woman could experience, next to being barren. This woman felt so much rejection by her own town's people that she made her visit to the town well to draw water at high noon, not in the early morning or the cool of the evening as others did.

As Jesus approached Sychar, this Samaritan woman's home town, He told His disciples that he was getting a little weary and wanted to rest on Jacob's well. Some of the disciples volunteered to go into town and buy lunch for everyone, but at least John, and possibly some of the others, stayed at the well with Jesus. We know John was there, because he is the only one of the four Gospel authors who included this story in his account of the gospel of Jesus Christ.

After most of the disciples headed into town for food and Jesus had sat on Jacob's well for a few minutes, along came this Samaritan woman to the well to draw water. She hesitated for a moment, after seeing Jesus on the well, then proceeded to get her water. She did not expect any type of trouble from this Jew, since most Jews would simply ignore the Samaritans around them.

But as she began to pull up the first vessel of water, Jesus broke the silence by speaking to her.

Jesus: (Enters at the appropriate time of the narration and sits on a prop made to look like the edge of the well or a chair that is facing upstage. The make-believe or prop-defined well should be positioned down-center stage, between the actors and the audience. Your legs will point upstage slightly, so turn your body so your face will be seen. Look down into the well, wave goodbye to the disciples, and glance around. When the woman comes in, establish eye contact with her, making her stop. Smile at her and never look away from her until instructed to do so.)

Woman of Samaria: (Follow the lead of the narrator, acting out what he reads slightly before he reads it. Make sure eye contact with Jesus makes you stop. Then proceed to the well cautiously. Mime tying a rope around the neck or handle of a big pot, and lower it down into the well. Bend over and stare intently down the well, and wait while the pot lays over on its side and begins to fill with water. Always mime holding the rope as long as the pot is down the well. Do all this with an uncomfortable air, trying to, but never successfully ignoring Jesus.)

Jesus: (Pause) Give me a drink?

Woman of Samaria: (Looks quickly at Jesus, then raises her body slowly and looks at Jesus seriously.) How is it that you, being a Jew, ask me—a woman of Samaria—for a drink? (now sarcastically bitter) I thought Jews have nothing to do with Samaritans. (Sigh and turn back to the business of pulling the pot out of the well, bending over once again.)

Jesus: (Stand and walk around behind her as though you are going to walk away. When you reach a couple of steps beyond her, stop, turn, and face her; touch your forefinger to your mouth; then point to her by only bending the wrist and shake the finger twice; then quickly withdraw the point.) If you knew the gift of God (pause) and who it is who asks you for a drink (turn a quarter away slowly, looking out), you would have asked Him for a drink (turn back to her smiling) and He would have given to you living water.

Woman of Samaria: (Glance quickly at Jesus after the last two words, by turning just the head, then raise and turn your whole body to face Jesus, keeping your eyes on Him. Speak condescendingly.) Sir, you have nothing to draw water with, and the well (gesture toward the well) is deep—from where, then, do you have this (sarcastically) living water? Are you greater than our father Jacob, who gave us this well and drank from it himself as did his children and his cattle? (Shake your head in disgust as you turn back to your work. Reach down and mime lifting a pot the final way out of the well.)

Jesus: (Step toward her with a slight smile.) Whoever drinks (Touch her hand closest to you.) of this water shall thirst again: But (Walk back around behind her, staying close; end with your face close to her face.) whoever drinks of the water that I shall give him shall never thirst; (Lean back slowly as you speak; let your smile build.) but the water that I shall give him shall be in him (pause) a well of water springing up into everlasting life.

Woman of Samaria: (Stand facing Jesus with fists on the hips, very sarcastic.) Sir, give me this water so that I do not thirst or have to come here to draw water again.

Jesus: (Turn slowly a quarter away from her.) All right. (Take two steps away from her, then turn and face her.) But first, go call your husband and come back so I can give it to both of you.

Woman of Samaria: (Embarrassed, turn a quarter away, look down, and wring hands) I (pause) have no husband.

Jesus: You have well said that you have no husband: (Turn slowly and look away as you speak.) For you have had five husbands in the past; and (Look back at her.) he whom you now have is not your husband, (Look away again.) so I guess in what you said you spoke truly.

Woman of Samaria: (React appropriately with a quiet gasp and hang your head to what Jesus has said. Then, slowly look up, revealing a good idea in your eyes. Say the next words slowly as you turn your face to Jesus.) Sir, I perceive that you are a prophet, a Holy man. (now quickly and confidently) Tell me, sir, there's something I've always wanted to ask a religious leader. Our fathers worshipped in this mountain (Gesture toward the mountain; use flattering, condescending tones.); but you Jews say that in Jerusalem is the place where men should worship. I was wondering, sir, (Tilt your head and flutter your eyes.) which is correct?

Jesus: (With all sincerity and love, looking into her eyes, touch her on the hand or the shoulder.) My dear lady, believe me, the hour is coming when you shall neither worship the Father in this mountain (Gesture toward the mountain.), nor at Jerusalem (gesture toward Jerusalem.). You see, you Samaritans worship a god that you do not know. We Jews at least know about the God we worship, for salvation is coming through the Jews. But the hour is coming, and now is when the true worshipers shall worship the Father in spirit and in truth. The Father is seeking this kind of worshiper to worship him. You see, God is a Spirit—and they who worship him must worship him in spirit (pause) and in truth.

Woman of Samaria: (Slowly lose eye contact with Jesus and turn your face away, showing bewilderment and deep thought. Take a couple of steps away from Jesus, shaking your head no. Say the next line still looking away, very labored with long pauses to show deep thought.) I know that the Messiah is supposed to be coming, who is called Christ, and that when He comes, He will be able to tell us everything.

Jesus: (Gently walk over to her and place your hand on her shoulder.) I (pause) that speak unto you am He.

Woman of Samaria: (Look quickly into Jesus' eyes. Begin to cry. As you sob to the point of uncontrollable, slowly bow your head, and sink to your knees, grabbing Jesus' robe about knee height.) My Lord! My Lord!

Jesus: (Gently reach down, and raise her to a standing position. Look straight into her eyes, with a smile on your face.) My daughter, (pause) your sins are forgiven.

Woman of Samaria: (Cry again, but change the sound to a joyful cry. Fall against Jesus' chest, as He embraces you as His child.)

Jesus: (Embrace her as a father would.)

(curtain or blackout)

Bibliography

Botterweck, G. Johannes, Helmer Ringgren, Heinz-Josef Fabry (Eds.). *Theological Dictionary of the Old Testament (Vol. V) (D. E. Green, Trans.)* (Grand Rapids: William B. Eerdmans Publishing Company, 1986).

Bright, Bill, *Have You Heard the Four Spiritual Laws?* (Peachtree City, GA: Bright Media Foundation and Campus Crusade for Christ, 2007). https://crustore.org/downloads/4laws.pdf.

Carswell, Eddie and Leonard Ahlstrom. *The Christmas Shoes.* Sony/ATV Songs LLC and WB Music Corp./Jerry's Haven Music, Reunion Records MPCD40512, 2000, compact disc.

Crabb, Lawrence J., Jr. *Institute of Biblical Counseling: Training Manual.* (Colorado, 1978).

Francisco, Don. *Love Is Not a Feeling.* Benson Music, 1984, accessed on October 29, 2017, https://www.youtube.com/watch?v=mKbHFMADh8Y.

Grace, Jamie, Toby McKeehan, Morgan Nichols, Chris Stevens. Beautiful Day. Capitol CDP 7 46381 2, 2013, compact disc.

"Human Brain Still Awake, Even During Deep Sleep," University of Liège, last modified October 17, 2008, accessed on July 3, 2014, http://www.sciencedaily.com/releases/2008/10/081008101740.htm.

Merriam-Webster.com. s.v. "good," accessed on February 3, 2017, https://www.merriam-webster.com/dictionary/good.

Nee, Watchman. *The Spiritual Man (Vol. One).* (New York: Christian Fellowship, Inc., 1977).

The Expanded Bible. (Nashville: Thomas Nelson Publishing, 2011).

Pratney, Winky. *The Babylonian Pattern.* (1972). Retrieved 2016.

"Sleep: A Dynamic Activity," National Institute of Neurological Disorders and Strokes, accessed February 3, 2017, http://www.ninds.nih.gov/disorders/brain_basics/understanding_sleep.htm#dynamic_activity.

Stone, Shamblin. *Biblical Worship.* (Bloomington: WesBow Press, 2012).

Strong, J. *Strong's Exhaustive Concordance of the Bible.* (Peabody: Hendrickson Publishers, 2007).

The Evolution Conspiracy, directed by R. Oakland (Jeremiah Films, 1988, 2009), DVD.

The Holy Bible, King James Version.

The Holy Bible, New International Version, (Colorado Springs: Biblica, Inc.,1973, 1978, 1984, 2011).

The Living Bible. (Carol Stream: Tyndale House Foundation, 1971).

The New King James Version. (Thomas Nelson, 1982).

Vine, W. E., Merrill F. Unger, William White Jr. *Vine's Complete Expository Dictionary of Old and New Testament Words,* accessed on February 3, 2017, http://www.ultimatebiblereferencelibrary.com/Vines_Expositary_Dictionary.pdf.

Webster, Noah. *American Dictionary of the English Language.* (Foundation for American Christian Education, Facsimile of the original 1828 edition, published in 1968).